Careers in Healthcare and Beyond

Careers in Healthcare and Beyond

Tools, Resources, and Questions to Prepare You for What's Next

Evelyn M. Lee

A PRODUCTIVITY PRESS BOOK

First published 2021
by Routledge
600 Broken Sound Parkway #300, Boca Raton FL, 33487

and by Routledge
2 Park Square, Milton Park, Abingdon, Oxon, OX14 4RN

Routledge is an imprint of the Taylor & Francis Group, an informa business

© 2021 Taylor & Francis

The right of Evelyn M. Lee to be identified as author of this work has been asserted by her in accordance with sections 77 and 78 of the Copyright, Designs and Patents Act 1988.

All rights reserved. No part of this book may be reprinted or reproduced or utilized in any form or by any electronic, mechanical, or other means, now known or hereafter invented, including photocopying and recording, or in any information storage or retrieval system, without permission in writing from the publishers.

Trademark notice: Product or corporate names may be trademarks or registered trademarks, and are used only for identification and explanation without intent to infringe.

A catalog record for this title has been requested

ISBN: 9781032039862 (hbk)
ISBN: 9781138626737 (pbk)
ISBN: 9781315222684 (ebk)

DOI: 10.1201/b22077

Typeset in Minion
by Deanta Global Publishing Services, Chennai, India

This book is dedicated to my mother, Faye Mok,

in honor of her hopes and dreams

Contents

Acknowledgments xi
About the Author xiii
Introduction xv

Chapter 1 Gathering Information 1
    In the Beginning, Mapping Out Your Journey 2
    The Early Years 3
    Developing Your Story 3
    Getting Started: Discovering Your 5Ws 5
        Who 5
        What 6
        Your College Major 7
        Your Major as a Path 7
        Looking Ahead 12
        Where 15
        When 16
        Why 17
    Building Your 5Ws 18
    Monitoring Your 5Ws as They Evolve 18
    Exploring Options 20
    Learn About Research 20
    Stay Informed About Job Trends 22
    Learning from Others 23
    Action Items 23
    In Closing 25

Chapter 2 Tools You Can Use, Getting Ready to Tell Your Story 27
    Before You Begin 28
    Your Resume—Getting Started 29
    Organizing Your Resume 31
    Resume Writing as Preparation for an Interview 35

Building Your Resume 36
Cover Letters 37
Social Media 38
Interviews 38
Preparing for Assessment Tests 41
Preparing for Interviews 41
Informational Interviews and Networking 42
Conversation Starters 45
Conversation Expanders 45
Questions for Yourself 46
Networking Opportunities 46
Finding Mentors 49
Action Items 50
In Closing 51

Chapter 3 Getting to Know and Trust Yourself 53
Getting Started—Six Squares Photo Collage 54
Experiential Learning 57
Your Learning Preference 59
Your 5Ws 60
Experiential Learning and Preferences in Action 60
Resource for Career Information 63
Self-Assessments 64
Learning About Yourself through Conversation with Others ... 66
Learning from the Past 68
Making Time to Listen 69
Not My Favorite Subject 69
Action Items 71
In Closing 71

Chapter 4 Becoming Comfortable with Uncertainty 73
Accepting Uncertainty 74
Staying Grounded 75
Being Prepared 78
Day-to-Day Uncertainty in Healthcare and Research 80

Contents • ix

    Doing the Work 80
    Taking Action... 82
    Problem Solving.. 84
    It's Okay to Ask 86
    Uncertainty, a Part of Being... 88
    Coming Full Circle 89
    Following My Heart 91
    Action Items 92
    In Closing.. 93

Chapter 5   Growth: Bridging the Gaps and
               Continuing to Learn 95

    The Gaps... 96
    I Would if I Had Time... 97
    What Do I Need to Know? 98
    What's in the Job Description? 99
    Shh ... No One Knows... 99
    To Advance or Transition Your Career 100
    Gaps in the Form of Time 100
    Ways to Bridge the Gaps... 101
    Dig In and Dig Deep 105
    Don't Have Any Gaps? 106
    Action Items 106
    In Closing.. 107

Chapter 6   Progress Leads to Success................................ 109

    Know Yourself, Know the Job 110
    Stay Informed 113
    Be Prepared to Pivot... 113
    How to Pivot 115
        Take a Personal Inventory 115
    Measures of Success 117
    Making Progress at Your Own Pace 121
    How You Do What You Do 123
    Action Items 123
    In Closing.. 124

References 127

Index 129

Acknowledgments

I have been fortunate to have interacted with so many people who have shaped the content and messages in this book. I thank them all for the privilege of being a part of their life and career journeys.

I am grateful for the opportunities I have had to work and serve. The healthcare and biopharmaceutical organizations that I have been a part of and the academic partners I have interacted with have provided me with ways to help people grow their careers and connect their skills and interests with work.

A special note of gratitude goes to those individuals who played a pivotal role, especially early in my career, by teaching me, guiding me, believing in me, and creating opportunities for me to gain professional experience. There is a placeholder in my heart for all of these individuals who supported me in so many different ways that made my career journey and exploration possible. Included amongst these individuals were my mentors, graduate school and graduate committee advisors, hiring managers, friends, and colleagues.

As I was contemplating ways that I could assist students and professionals in their career journeys, I was inspired by the work of Victor Saad, founder of Experience Institute. Attending his events, reading his newsletters, and watching his work progress reinforced to me that learning opportunities are essential, beginning early in one's career and extending throughout. I thank Victor for showing me there is always more we can do.

My sincere gratitude goes to the real people behind Chloe, Carlos, Leon, Otis, Mina, Hannah, Emma, and Jasmine who so generously gave of their time and wisdom and allowed me to share their stories with you. I am also grateful to those who have shared their personal stories with me as reflected in the character of Gabrielle.

I am thankful to the beta readers for the time they took to thoroughly read my manuscript and provide helpful feedback. Their responses were timely and highlighted additional content that would be beneficial for the reader. I am truly indebted to them for their sincere efforts.

I am especially appreciative for Dr. Jeffrey C. Bauer, who is a visionary and helps me see the world through a different lens. He has been a friend and supporter who encouraged me to share my story through an invitation to write this book. This book would not have been possible without his vote of confidence.

I would like to extend a heartfelt thank you to Kristine Rynne Mednansky at Taylor & Francis Group for her enthusiasm from the first time we spoke about this project. I am especially appreciative of her patience and support in making this idea to reality.

Bringing a book from concept to reality involves the efforts of more than just the author. I am very thankful for the efforts of Danielle B. Perlin-Good. It is through her dedicated efforts working with me that this book integrates my experience and that of others, while providing tactical guidance for the career journey. I am very appreciative of the editorial insights and experience that Susan Walker provided. She worked very much in sync with me, just like a writing partner.

I am very grateful to the team at Taylor & Francis Group and Deanta Global Publishing Services for their support of bringing this manuscript from draft to final copy, and for all of their attention to the details.

A special thank you to my father, my grandparents, aunts and uncles, friends and especially my family who held space for me throughout my career journey and during the time I was writing this book. Their words of support and encouragement were always timely.

About the Author

Evelyn M. Lee is married, has two young adult children and a dog, and she lives in the greater Chicago area. She is a PhD scientist with industry experience in research and development and human resources.

Evelyn received a Bachelor of Arts in Chemistry from Northwestern University and a PhD in Biochemistry from the University of Illinois at Chicago. Upon completing her PhD, she joined a global diversified healthcare company where she held positions in research and development, and human resources over the course of her career.

Having worked in the healthcare and biopharmaceutical industry throughout her career, she has extensive experience in recruiting , career navigation, especially in the areas of science, healthcare, and marketing. Evelyn started her HR career, in what was then referred to as the Internal Staffing Center, where she followed her passion for advancing science—leaving the lab bench and searching directly for just the right people for each job opportunity.

Evelyn has led strategic partnerships with universities, internship and summer research programs, and recruitment efforts for internship and entry-level opportunities for undergraduates, graduates, and healthcare professionals. In addition to the healthcare industry, she has also assisted professionals in career transitions in the insurance, finance, and manufacturing industries.

She has often been asked by students how she started her career, and thus while on sabbatical, Evelyn wrote this book to share her personal story, stories from those she has guided, and lessons they learned along the way.

Introduction

When I was young, I easily answered the question, *what do you want to be when you grow up?* I had dreams of becoming a doctor, and nothing in this world would have stopped me from achieving that goal. As I entered college, I maintained that aspiration, declaring myself as pre-med when I was a freshman at a large distinguished research university. However, in the midst of my junior year, I started to question my career direction.

Though I had a solid support network at home and at school, I felt incredibly lost and lonely when I started to challenge my original career plans. It seemed as though everyone else had post-graduation plans except me. People tried to help, but every bone in my body said, "You need to think through this alone."

I could no longer envision myself the same way I did as a freshman. This was my future. Whatever decision I made would require a huge personal commitment of time and resources. I couldn't quite articulate what I was feeling, but my anxiety levels were at an all-time high as I repeatedly asked myself, "What do I want to be when I grow up?"

I knew that I cared about people, their health, and their well-being. I wanted to work in healthcare. I wanted to understand the human body and the nature of diseases. These desires were clearly an homage to my childhood.

When I was nine years old, my mother passed away due to complications associated with lupus; she was just 32 years old. Ten years prior to the start of her illness, she had immigrated to the United States, excited to start a new life. Yet this life was cut short. She did not get to see her three children grow up. She did not have the opportunity to guide us as we entered different stages of life. She was not able to be a part of our weddings or meet her grandchildren.

My mother's early passing left me with a lingering sadness. I had to grow up quickly and was left pondering hundreds of questions about life, diseases, and ailments. And I felt like I needed to tackle the world on my own. My search for answers inspired an interest in healthcare and a desire to learn everything I could about how the human body functions.

After much soul-searching and countless conversations, I made the decision to pursue a PhD in Biochemistry. Years later, I accepted an opportunity to work for a global healthcare company, leveraging my science background. Over the next 20 years, I worked at this healthcare company across many functions—in research and development, marketing, and human resources. As a recruiter, I gained valuable insights into career trajectories through the lenses of scientists, pharmacists, doctors, engineers, and marketing and business professionals. I came to realize that hundreds of opportunities exist for someone with an academic background in STEM (Science, Technology, Engineering, and Math).

As my career journey continued, I came to a fork in the road and again I needed to make a decision about my next steps. This time I made a bold decision and took a sabbatical. During this time, however, I continued to guide both students and professionals in their search for careers. Students often asked me to assist them with their resumes and help them prepare for interviews. When I attended networking events, students were eager to learn about career options. Common questions included:

What are my career options if I want to work in healthcare?
How did you get a job in the healthcare industry?
What types of training and experience do I need to work in healthcare?

As these questions often came up during conversations, I made a personal commitment to help students and young adults understand more about themselves and advance their careers.

Thus, several months later I was delighted to receive an invitation from my alma mater to participate in "The Future of Careers in Healthcare: An Expert Panel." The three-member panel included an independent health futurist and medical economist, well-published and globally recognized for his expertise; a healthcare consultant, experienced in the insurance industry; and me, a PhD scientist and human resources professional with more than 20 years of experience in research and development and talent acquisition for a leading global healthcare company.

I had previously participated in panel discussions about careers; however, this one was different. The students were interested in learning about careers in healthcare from a general perspective. Many of the students who attended were either undecided or had not previously thought about working in healthcare, and now they wanted to understand the options.

Thus, the professor asked me to specifically share my career journey and the factors that motivated me and influenced my decisions. He also asked that I offer suggestions about how students could prepare for their career search.

As the students entered the room, their eyes were glued to their phones. Their minds were far away from the classroom, but I hoped to draw their attention when the discussion began. I remembered how it felt to be in college again. The collective uncertainty of the future came right back to me, and I related to these students wholeheartedly even before I spoke a word to them.

I gave these students the same advice I have given to both undergraduate and graduate students over the years:

> It's not easy to know when you make a choice—whether it's your major or your career—if you are going to like doing this work forever. However, if you start having conversations with people and discussing the questions you have, and then spend quiet time exploring your thoughts, you may get closer to finding a path that works well for you. The magical moment is when you arrive at a sense of peace with your academic choices and your next steps after graduation.

Having interacted with hundreds of students, scientists, and medical and healthcare professionals during the course of their career journeys, I knew this message would resonate with the students. Anyone can feel uncertain, lonely, and confused at the prospect of the future, so I was eager to share my experience with these students, just as I'm thrilled to share my insights with you in this book.

If your academic and career interests have led you in the direction of a STEM major, or even if they have not, your career options may include working in healthcare, science, engineering, or computer and information technology. The *Occupational Outlook Handbook* (www.bls.gov/ooh/) CareerInfo App available on Android or iPhone published by the U. S. Department of Labor lists more than a hundred descriptions in different categories. The healthcare category alone has more than 45 different occupational titles. Navigating the options and being certain you feel good about your decision take time and effort.

Colleges and universities are a source of many solid resources. Supportive alumni share experience and insights through classroom lectures and networking opportunities. Input from parents, family members, and friends can also be valuable. All these channels of information and advice are important. However, your career decision—though it can be painstakingly difficult—is a choice that you must strive to make for yourself.

If you've picked up this book, then you're clearly motivated, determined, and ready to explore your career options. Throughout our journey together, we will dig into key insights and practices that will enhance your journey. You will build confidence in your choices and enhance your self-awareness. You will learn to leverage your network to learn more about career options. You will also learn how to make the connections between your interests and job opportunities.

For many years, I believed that I was the only person who struggled as a young adult trying to choose a career. However, I continued to hear the same dilemmas from others about their own career decisions. The reasons to choose one career over another are numerous—the statistics, the salary, your parents, your siblings, personal experience, your talents, your dreams and aspirations, and more. Throughout our journey together, I will show you how to build the knowledge you need to make career decisions with added confidence, and provide you with tips and suggestions when telling your story. We will build your experience through the necessary steps and actions to ensure you are adequately prepared for your chosen career path. Your definition of a successful career may change based on what you learn about yourself and potential opportunities. This change is to be expected and celebrated. Prepare yourself to dig in for a challenging yet rewarding process.

Over the course of my career, I have observed that if you listen and pay close attention, there are six crucial steps for a deeper understanding of yourself, your career options, and the world around you. As you work through the steps in each chapter, my hope is that you find clarity, gain insights, and listen to your innermost thoughts. These steps come from my own experience—what I did well, and what I wish I knew when I was a young adult. These steps also come from the experience of healthcare professionals and college graduates who have shared their stories with me. I've included stories from actual students I have worked with who were highly motivated and willing to do the work needed to embark on their journeys. Though the names of the characters are fictitious, the stories are authentic and represent individuals and their career situations, questions, and lessons learned.

Please recognize that one person's journey is never the same as another's. From my experience and the experience of those whom I have guided, career progress differs based on individual needs, wants, and desires. Receive the guidance and these suggestions with grace, and know that these viewpoints are meant to spark your ideas and action. Apply the chapters to address questions you have in the sequence that best fits your needs.

Throughout this book, my ultimate goal is to help you explore options and navigate your career from where you are to where you want to be. As you progress through each phase, I hope you learn more about yourself, your career preferences, and attain a better understanding of what success looks like for you.

1

Gathering Information

What steps can I take, what things can I be thinking about, or what questions can I answer that would help me with my own career journey?

—Chloe

Starting out on your career journey can be like looking out onto a mountain range. On a clear day, you can see trees, spires, and mountains.

You want to get a closer view. This is what the beginning of a career journey can feel like, but how do you know where to begin?

IN THE BEGINNING, MAPPING OUT YOUR JOURNEY

When I was in high school and first started to think about my career journey, I thought about what I like to study. My favorite classes were the science and math parts of STEM (Science, Technology, Engineering, and Math). Since I had an inherent interest in understanding more about the human body and the nature of diseases, it made sense to me that I would be interested in becoming a doctor. When my mother was still alive, she told my grandmother that she wanted her children to grow up to become doctors or nurses. My brother was to become a doctor, and I, being a girl, was to become a nurse. That was the perception years ago.

Growing up, I didn't have much exposure to nurses, but I interacted with doctors quite often. My grandparents didn't speak English, so I needed to accompany them to assist with translating instructions from doctors. Based on my experience of a patient's perspective, I liked the work that a doctor did. It was meaningful to see how the doctor asked questions, learned about the patient's symptoms, and could prescribe medicines to help them feel better. This view was very simplistic, but it was based on my experience at the time, and it seemed like work I would enjoy doing.

Becoming a doctor seemed like a very reasonable career aspiration for me. I was studious, did well in science, and enjoyed helping and interacting with people. In retrospect, I can now say that though my mother envisioned me in a highly regarded profession, I don't think it was necessarily her expectation. From what I knew at the time, though, it seemed like a very reasonable career interest. With full support and encouragement from my family, I made the decision to embark on the journey to become a doctor.

Entering college, I chose to major in chemistry and I declared that I was pre-med. As a result, I would need to take the prerequisites for medical school. It worked out well since the requirements for my major and the prerequisites for medical school overlapped. Aside from the academic requirements and a few experiences visiting a doctor's office, at that time I did not realize what was involved in being a doctor.

I can now acknowledge that my exposure to what a doctor does on a day-to-day basis was very limited. At school, the basic science classes I took were all interesting, but I wasn't getting exposure to working in a hospital or patient setting. At home, discussions during family gatherings focused on either food or cars. I would see, hear, and come to understand the nuances of working in the food and auto industries because they were the two industries my family was most involved in. Though I would get together with my friends, they had their own interests and journeys to follow as well. From the beginning, it was clear that even though I received strong support and encouragement for my career choice, any decision I made would need to be based on my own understanding.

THE EARLY YEARS

I recall that it was a very good feeling to be starting college knowing what career I wanted to pursue. It allowed me to focus my attention on making the required decisions as a freshman in college. I needed to register for classes for my major and plan for the prerequisites needed for medical school. In my classes, it was easy to meet other students who were also interested in science and medicine. Many of us were pre-med, and we each had our own reasons for pursuing this academic track. Some students continued on their path to medical school. Others changed their minds, as early as their first year, and others, even later—during their junior or senior years.

Students I have interacted with range from feeling definitive about what they want to study to being completely undecided. Some, when asked what they wanted to do when they grew up, were perfectly comfortable saying, "I don't know." Whichever category you are in now, know that it will likely evolve because you are in school. During this learning phase, your experiences will shape your understanding, perspectives, and possibly even your interests.

DEVELOPING YOUR STORY

When I first started college, I felt like just one student among many. It was a very different feeling than when I was in high school and I had a group of friends, and the teachers knew me by name. As I sat in a large university auditorium, at times I wondered if my presence mattered. Would anyone notice whether I was there or not? Would my professor come to know me by my name? I found myself looking for connection and wanting to belong. If I were to ask each of the other students why they signed up for this class and how this decision fit into their career journey, they would each have a unique story.

In retrospect, no one explained to me that a freshman chemistry class and every other class I had selected and every decision I had made would be part of my story. Telling your story is easier when you can look back, but since we know you are on a career journey, let's explore how you can tell your story.

As we begin to look at the range of career options in healthcare, we will use an approach that is often used in journalism to formulate a story, and that is defining your 5Ws.

YOUR 5Ws

Who
What
Where
When
Why

When you start to recognize the 5Ws that inspire your career decisions, you will gain the clarity and confidence to make progress toward your interests. These words are simply to get the thought and discussion process started. I recommend using them to prompt your thoughts and establish parameters around the areas of interest you have identified.

The responses to these questions can be very simple words that capture your passion and describe what motivates you at any point in your career journey. Your responses will assist you in selecting your college major(s). They may help you make decisions about student activities you could be involved in or summer jobs/internships you could choose to pursue. If you don't have a clear answer yet, add this to your list of topics to explore.

As you search for your answers to the 5Ws, you will be closer to embracing your "yes, this is what I want to do." When you have embraced your "yes" and the career that you envision for yourself, then your desire to meet your own expectations will become more important than meeting others' expectations. Then you will be able to explain your 5Ws and your willingness to work toward your vision.

Over time, your vision may stay the same or it may change. For example, some people have always known what they wanted to do and they pursue this career with laser focus and persistence. For others, the journey may take more time as they learn and explore options to find what is right for them. I clearly belong to the second category.

I like to challenge myself to do new things, be in new environments, meet new people, adapt, and grow. Some might see this approach as unconventional or lacking direction, and I can understand how it may seem this way to a casual observer. Sometimes there may even be an unspoken stigma around changing your major, working in a job that is unrelated to what you studied, or taking your career in an unplanned direction. The reality is that people do make these changes.

Knowing yourself and understanding the reasons for your decisions—to the best of your knowledge— will help you navigate your career choices and make decisions for yourself. Keeping in mind the reasons for your decision can help you stay grounded, and even more importantly it helps you communicate your story.

GETTING STARTED: DISCOVERING YOUR 5Ws

You may just be starting your journey or perhaps you've been on your career journey for years. Understanding what motivates or inspires you will keep you moving forward. Realize though that sometimes the true answer does not become apparent, even to yourself, until later when you reflect on your experiences.

I'll share my 5Ws, where I started, and how I developed them over time.

Who

The answer to this question comes from your heart and your life experiences, and it may not be clear why one experience is more impactful than another. Your "who" can be

- A patient you have met who has created a lasting impression
- A family member, such as a parent, grandparent, or sibling

- A person, an organization, or a community that inspires you
- A population of people who have a certain disease or medical condition you want to help
- Someone you have never met, but someone whose story you have heard

Over time many people will touch your life or inspire you.

> My "who" in my first year of college: People with medical needs

What

The "what" question has many parts, and your answers to these parts may be consistent or they may seem to conflict. No answers are right or wrong; just select the ones that fit right now and know that they may change.

- What do you like to do?
- What is your major?
- What do you want to do for a career?
- What do you do best?
- What matters to you?
- What is your passion?
- What motivates you to want to learn?

During high school I was very interested in chemistry, so I selected it as my major in college. Because I was also a pre-med student, the overlapping course requirements reinforced my decision to major in chemistry. In fact, it made perfect sense to me.

If your "what" suggests healthcare careers, a STEM major is useful, but a major in the social sciences, education, or the arts can also lead to a career in healthcare. The *Occupational Outlook Handbook* published by the U.S. Bureau of Labor Statistics is a comprehensive resource for understanding the breadth of career options, and it provides an overview of the nature of work and the qualifications required for hundreds of occupations. It is available online and via the CareerInfo app for iOS and Android devices.

Using the search function to explore options can help you direct your focus. Some of the helpful information in this handbook includes:

- Median pay
- Typical entry-level education
- Job outlook (projection over next ten years)
- What people in this occupation do
- Work environment
- How to pursue this occupation
- Similar occupations

Your College Major

The selection of one college major over another is a personal decision. It may have been your favorite subject in high school, your favorite subject to study, or it may be a subject that is connected to or even required for your career decision. Academically, your major determines the number and types of classes and credit hours required to meet the college graduation requirements. Practically, though, your major helps prepare you for work in certain fields.

Your Major as a Path

In my experience looking at the paths that people have taken in their careers and with understanding the requirements for a job, there are three general approaches I have come to recognize. From a career perspective, it's like looking at a mountain range and trying to decide how you will approach it to get a closer look. To take a trip to an actual mountain range, you can choose many roads. To get to the mountain range that is your career, your major and all the activities, projects, jobs, internships, and experiences are part of your trip.

Sometimes it's hard to choose a major, but this is where I started, and this is what I stayed with as my undergraduate major.

My "what": Chemistry

For some occupations, such as nursing, the undergraduate path is (1) a bachelor's degree, (2) an associate's degree, or (3) a diploma from an approved program. The same approach applies to other disciplines, such as education or finance. Some jobs/occupations have very specific requirements or certifications. The approach to these occupations is like that in Figure 1.1. There are several options—all headed in one direction toward the destination of becoming a registered nurse, an educator, or a certified public accountant. These occupations may allow some flexibility in selecting majors, but there are generally accepted approaches to be qualified for these jobs.

Other jobs allow more flexibility in selecting the major, but they require specific prerequisites. For example, to qualify and be considered for some postgraduate programs, including medical school, law school, and pharmacy school, certain prerequisites must be met. College students may describe themselves as pre-med, pre-law, or as being in a pre-pharmacy program. If you are a STEM major, you may find yourself on this path as well, where your undergraduate major may lead to your pursuit of a job, a professional graduate program, or advanced/graduate studies in the same

FIGURE 1.1
Careers with well-defined requirements.

Gathering Information • 9

or another discipline, as shown in Figure 1.2. In these scenarios, there are multiple entry points and options to continue on this journey.

For some students, a major is just one component leading to a career. They may have many talents and interests and be willing to do different kinds of work. If you are in this group, you can incorporate your studies and interests while developing your skills and talents. You might start your journey by looking for the intersection between your studies (major), your skills and talents (what you are good at), and your interests (what you like to do). You may or may not know how to describe your career goal at this point. You may also have not identified a specific occupation or title. But in your heart, you would have a sense of what you are searching for. Your journey would look more or less like Figure 1.3, and it would have even more entry points and options.

As illustrated by these three different scenarios, having a thoughtful approach and making timely decisions could make your journey smoother since delays in your decisions could impact the amount of time you are in

FIGURE 1.2
Careers with multiple entry points and options.

10 • Careers in Healthcare and Beyond

FIGURE 1.3
Keeping career options open.

school. See Table 1.1 for a comparison of different approaches to looking at your major.

Starting with the end in mind, the first goal upon entering college should be completing your degree, because a degree opens doors for you. Setting expectations upfront for yourself and understanding how your selection of major might impact your progression after graduation may influence how you approach your decisions in college.

Approach 1 is well-defined, and the requirements are clear. Approach 2 offers some flexibility, and you make choices with your goal in mind. Approach 3 describes you if you feel that you may change the kind of work you want to do relative to your major. Even if you have completed your degree when you change your mind, you still have made a major accomplishment. A college degree is more often a job requirement than a degree in a specific major. The goal of any of these approaches is to find the intersection between your academic and career interests, taking into consideration your skills and talents—the things you feel naturally good at doing.

According to the U.S. Department of Education (2012/14), within three years of initial enrollment, about 30 percent of undergraduates in associate's and bachelor's degree programs who declared a major changed their major at least once. About one in ten students changed their major

TABLE 1.1

Comparing the Effort Needed to Plan for Career Journey

	Your Major as It Relates to Next Steps	Level of Additional Effort Needed to Define Next Steps
1	Major is a requirement for specific job	Minimal, follow the academic, training, and certification requirements
2	Major in a STEM or non-STEM area	It depends on whether you are looking for a job or going to graduate school aligned directly with the academic field of study; if continuing with graduate school, admissions tests may be part of the application process
3	Major in a STEM or non-STEM area, interested in applying your academic training, but not certain what is of interest to you	Plan ahead for extra effort to find that "right next step" that is a cross-section of your studies, skills, and interests

more than once. Selecting your major is one of the most important decisions you'll make in college since you will be making a commitment to your major for at least three to four years of your life.

Your college major does not define you, your career, or your success; however, it does become the starting point for all of your career conversations. While you are in college, your major and your GPA are in the first few lines of your resume. Thus, try to select a major that aligns with your career goals. If you are not sure, pick a subject that you really like, because with any major, you still have many career options. It is a matter of where your starting point is and how much additional schooling or training you need to do the work you wish to do.

College majors are often categorized as STEM majors (Science, Technology, Engineering, and Math) or non-STEM majors. Additionally, for some healthcare jobs, obtaining a major in the specific discipline is an academic requirement. For example, a bachelor's degree in nursing is a requirement to be a nurse, in addition to state licensing. See Table 1.2 for examples of the areas of study associated with each major.

Chemistry was my favorite subject in high school, so I wanted to study it in college. At the time, I didn't know exactly how I would apply my knowledge of chemistry on the job, but I thought it would be beneficial for me. Because I liked science, any job or postgraduate studies I might pursue would likely involve an understanding of molecular structure and chemical interactions.

TABLE 1.2

Examples of the Areas of Study Associated with Different Categories of Majors

Type of Major	Areas of Study
STEM majors (Science, Technology, Engineering, Math)	Biological and Agricultural Sciences, Physics, Physical Sciences, Computer and Information Sciences, Management Information Systems, Chemical Engineering, Biomedical Engineering, Electrical Engineering, Mathematics, Statistics, Actuarial Science
Non-STEM majors	Education, Finance, Economics, Accounting, Business Economics, International Relations, Marketing, Entrepreneurial Studies, Foreign Languages, Communications, Music, English, Business, Political Science, Psychology
Healthcare majors	Nursing, Pre-Veterinary, Pre-Dentistry, Pre-Pharmacy, Food and Nutrition

You can choose any major and still work in an area that you hope for. Although trends and statistics show that STEM majors often work in STEM occupations and non-STEM majors, in non-STEM occupations, that's not always the case. Some STEM majors work in non-STEM-related occupations, and just the same, some non-STEM majors work in STEM or healthcare-related jobs. The correlation between the type of major and the type of occupation is represented in an interactive graphic published by the U.S. Census (Figure 1.4).

Figure 1.4 shows data reflecting STEM and non-STEM majors and the occupation groups they work in. Most notably, the graphic shows that people with either STEM or non-STEM majors work in healthcare. However, most STEM occupations are filled by STEM majors.

Looking Ahead

While selecting a major, consider the minimum degree requirements for the healthcare occupation. Review your selection with your college or university and then map out the academic curriculum so that you have an understanding of the road ahead. With an idea of the professions that require advanced degrees, start to keep in mind the number of years in school you may need before you are working in your desired field. See Table 1.3.

Working in healthcare, you are in positions that can help people maintain health and improve their well-being, such as those listed in Table 1.3.

Gathering Information • 13

(a) STEM majors working in Healthcare

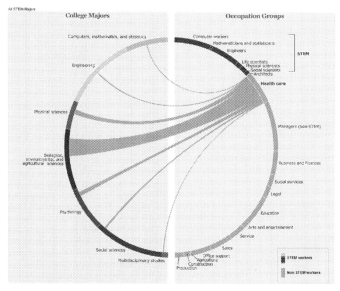

(b) Non-STEM majors working in Healthcare

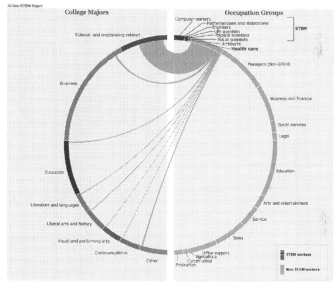

FIGURE 1.4
Data from Interactive Graph generated by U.S. Census data shows that those working in healthcare jobs come from both STEM and non-STEM majors. (a) STEM majors working in healthcare; (b) non-STEM majors working in healthcare. *Source*: census.gov/dataviz/visualizations/stem/stem-html.

TABLE 1.3

Degree Requirements for Healthcare Occupations

Minimum Degree Requirements*	Healthcare Occupations
Doctoral or professional degree	Physician, surgeon, dentist, pharmacist, physical therapist, veterinarian
Master's degree	Physician assistant, nurse practitioner, nurse anesthetist, nurse midwife, occupational therapist, genetic counselor, speech/language pathologist
Bachelor's degree	Registered nurse, athletic trainer, clinical laboratory technologist, dietician, nutritionist
Associate's degree	Clinical laboratory technician, radiologic and MRI technologist, respiratory therapist, veterinary technologist

*Some jobs in healthcare do not require an associate's or a bachelor's degree. These include pharmacy technician, phlebotomist, medical records and health information technician, medical assistant, and medical transcriptionist.

There is a separate use of the word "healthcare" in the description of businesses and services that are grouped as part of an industry. Thus, in day-to-day terms, one may say they work in the healthcare industry, if they work for a company that manufactures healthcare products. However, with respect to those who are healthcare providers, there is a distinction between working in healthcare as a physician or a nurse practitioner versus working as a scientist or an engineer in the healthcare industry. Table 1.4 provides examples of jobs that provide products or services that support the healthcare industry; however, those working in these jobs are not necessarily considered healthcare workers.

If you are not certain about what you want to major in, look through the list of course offerings and be open to trying new options. At the same time, start to look through the *Occupational Outlook Handbook* (or CareerInfo app), paying attention to the details. Sections both online and in the app offer information that is quite pertinent when making a decision on a career. Comprehensive information on each of these areas may be helpful as you are deciding on career options and majors:

- Occupation titles for many different groups
- Job summaries
- Education requirements for entry-level position
- Median pay

TABLE 1.4

Examples of Roles and Work that Provide Healthcare Products and Services

Academic Studies/Major	Where	What	Who/Why Impact/Influence on Products and Services That Are Useful in Healthcare and the Healthcare Industry
Scientist	Lab, healthcare company, biotech	Research scientist	Problem solving, understanding disease, data
Engineer	Hospital, biotech, start-up	Biomedical engineer	Improve, maintain, and design products that help people in their quest for well-being
Teacher	Classroom, home	Home teaching	Helping students with disabilities or medical conditions learn
Lawyer	Office, courtroom	Healthcare law	Help people receive quality care

- Description of the work
- Work environment
- How to become this occupation
- Job outlook for the next ten years

These details are all very useful in comparing occupations, and they give you an idea about which occupations are projected to need more workers in the future.

Where

As you learn about different careers, the question of "where" you might work becomes important. "Where" can include:

- Geographic location
  - Country, city or state, urban vs. rural environment
  - Stay close to home or move for the opportunity
- Work environment
  - Hospital or clinical setting, laboratory, business office, home office
  - Typical day, communication style, people you are around

- Organization type and size
  - Academic institution, large company, small business
  - Structured, casual, open

Not sure if you have a preference? Start to explore and take advantage of opportunities to speak with people about their work locations. Ask for opportunities to job shadow and see where and how people do their work.

> My "where" when I was in college: Laboratory, working with others

When

Questions around "when" help you frame the timing you have in mind for your life. Although you can't plan every aspect of building a career, mental preparedness comes into play.

I remember exactly where I was when I realized that I wanted to continue my education after college: I was walking across a parking lot on campus. I still had so much more to learn. I wanted to understand how to make better decisions, and I wanted to learn more about the human body and what causes disease states. Though there were jobs posted for graduating seniors to consider, I didn't feel ready to venture into the unknown. By this time, I had also started to question whether medical school was right for me. Even though I didn't know exactly what I wanted to do, I did know that I wanted to continue my education and that I would be in school for at least another four years. The other reason I wanted to continue straight through to graduate school was that I didn't trust that I would want to go back to school if I left academia.

Since my studies were in the field of science, I also prepared myself for understanding the impact of these decisions on my personal life. Continuing my education and pursuing advanced studies meant that I would be a working parent. It was just a mental note that I would have to have a strong commitment to my work and career and would need to balance this with family. There were no plans at the time; I was just thinking ahead. When approaching thoughts about "when," consider the following areas:

- Number of years in school
- Timing of your education, now or later

- Continuing your education in sequence or over time
- The options you have to choose from
- Other items on your wish list
- After you understand the logistics

Graduate school is not for everyone though, and I have spoken with many students who have felt that way. They felt like they had been in school long enough and they wanted to be in the world of work. They wanted to meet new people, learn new things, and see how far they could go with what they have learned. If you feel this way as well, the good news is that a graduate degree is not required for all jobs in healthcare or in all STEM or non-STEM-related opportunities. By looking at both internship and full-time job postings before you apply for jobs, you'll start to understand the type of skills and experience needed for positions that seem interesting to you.

Even if a job seems far removed from what you are studying, take note of the responsibilities that catch your attention. Start looking at job postings and descriptions before you are actively seeking a job. Getting familiar with job postings early in your career will help you identify the education, skills, and experience needed for your career. Whether you are thinking about a job, graduate school, or following your entrepreneurial vision, understanding the skills needed to be successful can guide your decisions.

My "when": After graduate school

Why

The reasons you are inspired to do what you do all make up your "why." Your reasons might include:

- It's interesting
- Someone you know does something similar and you want to learn more about it
- Helping people is a priority for you
- This work is needed in the world, and you want to help fill that need

18 • *Careers in Healthcare and Beyond*

- A family member, friend, or perhaps even a stranger has inspired you
- Maybe you are not sure why, but you feel like it is right for you

> My "why": I care about people's health and well-being

BUILDING YOUR 5Ws

In the beginning, you may or may not have identified all of your 5Ws. As you are trying to formulate your 5Ws, see what piques your interest by reading and attending seminars, workshops, and panel discussions on a range of topics. Get to know your professors and talk with them about what you are learning in the classroom and how it translates to real life.

That's actually how I discovered the research that I wanted to work on in graduate school. We were learning about magnetic resonance spectroscopy in class. When I visited the professor during office hours, we started talking about it further, and then he mentioned that magnetic resonance principles were being used to develop instruments that could collect data from humans *in vivo*. I found it so interesting that I did research to understand how it was being applied to medicine. MRIs are now a routine part of healthcare screening; however, years ago, this technology was still in its research phase and I got to experience it. Wanting to do this research also led me on the path to pursuing my PhD.

MONITORING YOUR 5Ws AS THEY EVOLVE

It is common that a person's career direction and interests will evolve. Your knowledge and expertise may deepen in an area that you find to be of great interest, or you may start to broaden your scope of experience. And, your 5Ws may also change over time.

When I was in college, I worked at a research lab affiliated with a medical center. Table 1.5 shows how my 5Ws evolved over time.

TABLE 1.5
The Progression of My 5Ws Over the Course of My Career

5Ws	Freshman in College	Junior in College	Senior in College	After Completing PhD	Before Transition to Human Resources
Who	Patients	Patients	Patients	Global patient population	Global patient population
What	Doctor	Not sure	Research	Program manager	Recruiting science, medical and business talent for global healthcare company
Where	Hospital	Not sure	Laboratory	Laboratory in global healthcare company	Global healthcare company
When	After med school	After four more years of school, not sure which program	After graduate School	After completing PhD	After eight years in research and development
Why	Wanted to help people feel better	Wanted to understand why people got sick	Wanted to be involved in finding answers	Wanted to be involved in developing products that would make a difference in people's lives	Wanted to be involved in finding people who could contribute to developing new products

Just as my 5Ws changed over time, yours will most certainly as well. As you are in these early stages of your career, remember that depending on the academic or job decisions you make, either there will be well-defined guidelines and expectations, or you will need to set your own course and explore, learn, and search for what is right for you.

EXPLORING OPTIONS

- Visit colleges and university websites to learn about the academic programs and research programs.
- Ask how people have applied their undergraduate majors or graduate studies and the types of work they have done to advance their careers.
- Take yourself on a virtual research adventure and learn about healthcare initiatives around the world.
- Start to follow publications that discuss farming, agriculture, and sources of food and nutrition to understand the impact that foods have on health.

LEARN ABOUT RESEARCH

There are many types of research, some of which involve doing research in the laboratory, with patient involvement to varying degrees. Career options in research can best be described through the translational science spectrum (https://ncats.nih.gov/translation/spectrum#preclinical-research), which represents each stage of research along the path from the biological basis of health and disease to interventions that improve the health of individuals and the public. See Figure 1.5.

- *Basic research* involves scientific exploration that can reveal fundamental mechanisms of biology, disease, or behavior. Every stage of the translational research spectrum builds upon and informs basic research.
- *Preclinical research* connects the basic science of disease with human medicine. During this stage, scientists develop model

interventions to further understand the basis of a disease or disorder and find ways to treat it. Testing is carried out using cell or animal models of disease; samples of human or animal tissues; or computer-assisted simulations of drug, device, or diagnostic interactions within living systems.
- *Clinical research* includes studies to better understand a disease in humans and relate this knowledge to findings in cell or animal models; testing and refinement of new technologies in people; testing of interventions for safety and effectiveness in those with or

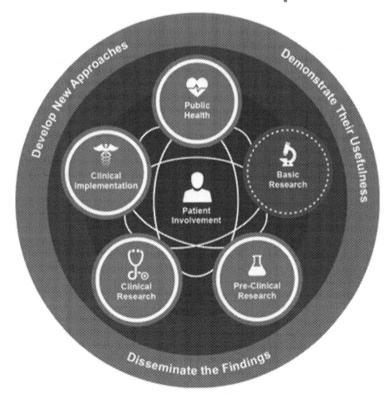

FIGURE 1.5
NIH translation science spectrum. *Source*: https://ncats.nih.gov/translation/spectrum#preclinical-research.

> without disease; behavioral and observational studies; and outcomes and health services research. The goal of many clinical trials is to obtain data to support regulatory approval for an intervention.
> - *Clinical implementation* is a stage of translation that involves the adoption of interventions that have been demonstrated to be useful in a research environment into routine clinical care for the general population. This stage also includes implementation research to evaluate the results of clinical trials and to identify new clinical questions and gaps in care.
> - *Public health* is where researchers study health outcomes at the population level to determine the effects of diseases and efforts to prevent, diagnose, and treat them. Findings help guide scientists working to assess the effects of current interventions and to develop new ones.
>
> Source: *Definitions provided by NIH. See source for Figure 1.5.*

If research seems to be of interest to you, there are some areas of research where an undergraduate degree is the basic requirement. Other areas of research involve obtaining a master's degree or a Doctor of Philosophy (PhD). Research may be done in an academic, a hospital, or an industry setting. After completing a PhD, options include continuing to gain research experience through a postdoc or finding a job in industry. Postdoc experience is often preferred, but not always required.

STAY INFORMED ABOUT JOB TRENDS

Regularly reviewing the employment projections (www.bls.gov/emp/) section of *Occupational Outlook Handbook* online or with the CareerInfo app (see References at the end of the book) will help you identify job trends. The numbers posted will show the percentage of increase or decrease in job opportunities over a projected timeframe, such as over a ten-year period. Though job availability and trends should not overly inform your career decision, understanding the job opportunities anticipated when you are looking for a job could help you make better decisions.

If current trends in healthcare (Bauer, 2020) indicate there will be an increased need for advanced practitioners, would these opportunities be of interest to you? Licensing and certification vary by state; the role of an advanced practitioner is to be part of a medical care team. The titles for advanced practitioners include:

- Nurse practitioners (NPs)
- Certified registered nurse anesthetists (CRNAs)
- Certified nurse midwives (CNMs)
- Clinical pharmacists (PharmDs)
- Doctors of physical therapy (DPTs)
- Doctors of clinical psychology (PsyDs)

These roles involve serving the patient as part of a larger clinical team.

LEARNING FROM OTHERS

Sometimes we think that job shadowing needs to be something formal where you ask someone if you can go to work with them for a day. Honestly, shadowing someone can happen quite casually. You might have a coffee chat with someone, or talk with someone who lives in your dorm. Ask them about their work and listen to their stories about their work or projects. When are they working their hardest? When do they seem exhilarated? When does it seem stressful? Depending on the location where they work, you might be able to stop in for a visit, take a quick tour, or meet them for lunch.

ACTION ITEMS

1. Start to document your 5Ws on Table 1.6. Review and update these every 3–6 months.
2. Visit the *Occupational Outlook Handbook* and select two occupations that you are currently considering. Use the information to compare the positions using a template like that in Table 1.7.

TABLE 1.6

Use This Template to Start Tracking Your 5Ws

5Ws	Today	Date	Date	Date	Date
Who					
What					
Where					
When					
Why					

Notes to self, including areas to explore, questions to address, action needed:

TABLE 1.7

Template for Comparison of Two Positions Described in the Occupation Outlook Handbook

	Occupation #1	Occupation #2
Median pay		
Entry-level education		
Job outlook		
What people in this occupation do		
Work environment		
How to pursue this occupation		
Similar occupations		

IN CLOSING

As you are formulating your 5Ws, read and attend seminars, workshops, and panel discussions about careers. Be curious about everything and everyone you meet. Ask questions. Begin by asking people about the type of work they do and how they got their first job. Try to understand what types of studies were important in their careers. Take advantage of opportunities for job shadowing to get a closer understanding of people and their work.

Understand that there's no "right" way to answer your 5Ws. There's only your way as you start your own career journey. As you look at these responses, you can see the range of experiences and timing and come to the realization that the answers may not all come at once. You may look outwards and plan a trek toward one destination only to find another path or a stop that catches your attention. Your answers will grow and change with time. Various conditions may influence your decisions; however, you can always find your way back to your preferences through your 5Ws. How might your 5Ws story begin?

2

Tools You Can Use, Getting Ready to Tell Your Story

I want to understand how I can use my training and skills and apply them in a way that makes a difference in the world.

—Chloe

The best time to create a resume is when the idea first crosses your mind. You may not need it right at that moment; however, putting your accomplishments on paper is the best way to start. Once you have prepared

DOI: 10.1201/b22077-2

your first draft, review your resume at the start of each school year and again at the end, adding updates during the course of the year. Think of your resume as a living document.

The content of your resume may change during the course of the school year. It would provide the basis for your career conversations and become a reflection of the decisions, opportunities, and commitments you have made over time. Your resume is a reflection of your skills, experience, and talents, and your willingness to work, learn, and grow. As you prepare, keep in mind your 5Ws as they will be reflected in the content you create and the story you tell about yourself.

You can communicate your story through different formats and opportunities:

Written: resume, cover letter
Conversational: networking, informational interviews, formal interviews
Social: LinkedIn (formal) and all other social media channels (informal)

BEFORE YOU BEGIN

As you start the first draft of your resume, I suggest keeping two versions. One version has everything you have done, including all your awards and your activities. Consider this first version your master list and a working document that you use to keep a running list of all your professional and personal accomplishments. This one is only for you. It becomes a great study guide as you prepare for interviews as well since it summarizes everything you have done.

As you prepare your resume, cover letter, LinkedIn and other online profiles, and even as you prepare for interviews, reviewing this list reminds you of the many things you have done. Then when the need arises you can select what to include and incorporate into a specific resume or conversation.

Chloe, who I first met before her senior year, wished she had known about a master list. She was thinking more seriously about next steps after graduation and needed to pull out her resume and update it. Without a master list that is kept up to date, it is very easy to forget or simply disregard as unimportant some of the work you have done. In addition, remembering what you did and the exact dates you did it can become a challenge. Think of the master list as a life journal, and a way to reflect back on the experiences you have gained over time. The list will come in handy especially if you are in an interview or if someone asks about situations that you have been in. For example, if you had babysitting jobs, and you find yourself applying for a position involving youth, you can refer to those jobs. Or if you were a volunteer who helped coach a soccer team, you can use this experience as an example of your ability to teach and help others. I realize some of these examples may seem like a stretch. In the beginning, when you are trying to convey your abilities and potential, your early work and volunteer experiences are a good place to start. Over time you will have more formal examples, or you may enjoy going back to these early experiences that taught you skills beyond the classroom.

YOUR RESUME—GETTING STARTED

Start by looking into all the resources that are available at your school. Find out if the career center provides templates and guidelines or workshops and tips on how to write a resume. People at your school may be available to help you review your resume once you have it drafted. Your resume is not just a paper due in your English class. It is a document that stays with you for many years. Over time you will add and remove content (only remove content from your current resume, not your master list), so becoming familiar with writing a resume will be helpful. Knowing who you can approach for help is a great starting point. Having multiple people review your resume and ask you questions helps you realize what you might need to clarify or what might be missing.

Resume Tips

- At the top of the page: Your name, school email address, and phone number
- LinkedIn profile address: URL specific to your profile
- Number of pages: One, with a margin of close to 1" on all sides

- White space: Keep it easy to read, i.e., 80 percent text
- Categorize your accomplishments and then organize them using headers; you may combine some categories as:
  - Education (include anticipated graduation date and GPA)
  - Internships
  - Work experience
  - Technical experience, skills, certificates
  - Leadership roles
  - Extracurricular activities and sports
  - Community service and volunteering
  - Awards or other recognition

Select a format for your resume that is easy to edit. Your school's career center may advise a specific format, which will help you get started. The most important point part of writing a resume is to make the information easy to understand, concise, and accurate. When you show your resume to someone, they will have questions and want to learn more about what you have done. In turn, you will want to spend your time talking about the great work you have done rather than the details around the dates and logistics.

When Chloe and I were reviewing her resume, we set aside enough time to review her resume line by line. Though her resume had been updated each year, now that she was looking for a full-time opportunity, it made sense to place more scrutiny on each item in her resume. At this point, she had just about filled every space on the page with text, so we needed to go through each section of her resume to review and reorganize. Chloe had done so much over the last few years, we needed to determine which items to keep, remove, or add in.

GENERAL RESUME GUIDELINES

- You may keep accomplishments from high school in your freshman or sophomore year in college.
- As you progress from your sophomore to your junior and senior years in college, use more of your resume space to describe your college experience.

> - If jobs you had in high school taught you transferable skills, you can list the skill and briefly provide the context on your resume or discuss it in a cover letter or interview. For example, you might include working in retail (customer service), responsibility for social media posts (marketing), or volunteering at a hospital (patient interactions).

Preparing your resume takes time, even if you already have a draft. When Chloe decided to update her resume, she was surprised that it took her several hours to update and add her most recent internship to her resume. It was important to add her latest internship assignment and classroom projects to her resume. To keep the content to one page, we needed to review and select which items to retain, combine, or perhaps even eliminate. For example, at some point, even though you benefited from the jobs you had in high school, you may choose to remove them from your resume.

ORGANIZING YOUR RESUME

Even though resume templates are available, how you choose to organize your content depends on what you will include, and how much content you have for each category. Try to avoid having just one item in a category. Group similar items so that there are two or three items under each header.

Chloe created the first draft of her resume in high school and has been adding academic awards, accomplishments, campus activities, and internship experience every few months. Since she started taking more advanced engineering classes, she also added a skills section to her resume, capturing both technical and IT experience. It had been a few months since she last looked at her resume. As she pulled it up, she dreaded the need to review and revise it again. She wanted to include lots of information, but the resume was getting too long. Chloe also suspected that her resume was too condensed. The margin on each side was only half an inch, and she didn't like the way it looked. It just didn't seem professional. Yet each time Chloe asked someone at the career center for feedback, she was told it looked good, so she did not make any changes. When I told her that the margins were too narrow, she absolutely agreed. We reviewed and streamlined the content, so we could create wider margins and increase the white space on the paper. Though it took time to make the changes, Chloe was much happier with her resume's revised format.

Chloe had a good resume overall, and her content reflected the experience of a student majoring in biomedical engineering. She had included relevant examples of class projects and summer internships at well-established research institutions. She had a combination of administrative and office skills as well as technical skills. Her GPA was well-above average, and she was involved in activities on campus. The resume had no typos, and the descriptions of each project were reasonably clear.

As you build the content for each of your bullet points in the resume, focus on simplicity and clarity. This one-page document provides the reader with a synopsis of everything you want to tell them about yourself, and everything they want to know about you.

KEY CONTENT FOR A RESUME

- Education
  - School name and department
  - Degree (completed or anticipated) and corresponding date
  - Major, minor, or any concentrations, and GPA
  - Certificates and training (can be under education or technical skills)
- Experience (these categories and activities may be in separate sections or combined depending on the number in each category)
  - Internships (paid or unpaid, related to career or academic major)
  - Research
  - Jobs (general work experience)
  - Academic or course projects
- Skills and Technical Experience
  - Laboratory
  - Software, programming, or design
  - Language skills (if fluent in more than one language)

- Awards and Special Recognition
  - Academics awards or dean's list
  - Honor societies
- Campus Activities
  - Clubs or student groups
  - Athletics
  - Arts, theatre, and music

Think of your experiences as being curated for your resume. Though activities are grouped and listed in chronological order, your resume is also not simply a sequence of activities. You want to show a progression of professional development and an expansion in the scope of your responsibilities. They show you have gained the knowledge and experience needed to do the work in the job description. Your accomplishments and campus and leadership activities can highlight the level of commitment and effort you put into your work.

Invite people to review and provide feedback on your resume. Take advantage of opportunities to ask for input from trusted family members, career advisors, professors, and alumni. Select people who have at least a general understanding of your work and studies. Invite these reviewers to tell you what is clear and what may not be clear. Take time to tell your resume reviewers what you would want someone to know about each bullet point and ask if they have the same impression based on what you have written.

If possible, ask for a face to face meeting to review your resume so you can see their reaction. It's like watching someone do a taste test. Is there an instant response, such as *This tastes great*? Or does the reviewer take a moment and ask *What flavor is this again?* If they are pausing and rereading certain lines, it may indicate a lack of clarity in certain sections.

TIPS FOR ADDING CLARITY TO YOUR RESUME
- Determine how to categorize your lab, technical, and general computer skills.
- Add certifications and training that demonstrate advanced knowledge.

- If your activities are listed by year, describe jobs you work intermittently, such as summer jobs or jobs during the school year, describe them as such, rather than listing them multiple times.
- Show progression in skills and experience, while avoiding duplicate content.
- To keep resume at one page, adjust content on an ongoing basis; allocate more space for more recent experience and shorten descriptions for earlier activities.

You may need several rounds of edits before you are comfortable with your resume, but it is worthwhile to spend the time to ensure the sequence of events and the description of your activities are clear. This way, as a recruiter or hiring manager is reviewing your resume, their focus is on your experience rather than trying to understand nuances in the content of your resume.

As you build your resume, in addition to the content and the clarity, see if you have gained the experiences you need (or want) to be prepared for your future. For example, if you have done research on campus during the summer two years in a row, would you want to consider an internship in a hospital or in the healthcare industry during your third summer? Have your experiences helped you gain clarity on your 5Ws?

Reviewing your resume presents an opportunity to reflect on some of your experiences. When you look over your list of achievements and think about all of your jobs, it may feel like you have been in a whirlwind. Connecting the dots will help you tell your story.

Chloe and I reviewed her resume to include words that were descriptive and offered clarity, especially for positions that were not year-round, so some positions, especially those she held for multiple years, had qualifiers such as "during the school year" or "during the summers."

If you are pursuing a career in science, engineering, or medicine, you may be asked to present a Curriculum Vitae (CV) in addition to or in place of your resume. In the medical and scientific community, a CV is often preferred. It reflects a progression over the course of a lifetime of medical and/or scientific accomplishments. Unlike a resume, there is no limit to the number of pages for a CV.

> **KEY CONTENT FOR A CV**
>
> - Name and Contact Information
>   - Full mailing address
>   - Office, phone number, email
> - Education
>   - Degree (completed or anticipated) and corresponding date
>   - Include titles for dissertations
> - Honors and Awards
> - Publications
> - Work Experience
> - Teaching Experience
> - Conference Presentations
> - Campus Service
> - Community Service
> - Internships
> - Leadership
> - Languages

Additionally, a CV includes a detailed yet succinct description of research grants one has been awarded and research projects, fellowships, scientific training, and certifications. For an experienced research scientist, this document can be well over 50 pages long.

RESUME WRITING AS PREPARATION FOR AN INTERVIEW

Preparing your resume is an exercise you start on your own; however, to get the most of this exercise, it is good to start reviewing the resume with others as soon as it is ready. The first assessment of a resume is its clarity. Is it easy to read? Does it look nicely formatted? Once you get past this general feedback, it's time to dig into the details, because you only have one or two lines to communicate your knowledge and experience. Be selective and clear in the words you use, ensuring that you use keywords and terminology that accurately reflect your knowledge. Sometimes you will hand your resume to someone you meet with, but when you submit your resume online, an automated process using artificial intelligence is most likely the first reviewer of your resume.

When Chloe asked friends and family for feedback on her resume, one section made them pause because they did not fully understand the content. Specifically, in addition to her major, she had obtained a certification that is a unique program offered by her school.

This was an "aha" moment for Chloe and I. As we discussed this certificate, Chloe explained that she developed a keen interest in this area—design—and made an extra effort to gain experience so that she could do more of this work when she graduated. Based on the importance of this certificate to her education, we repositioned this experience on her resume and moved the certificate from the technical skills section and placed it in the row just under her academic major. This new positioning highlighted the significance of completing this certificate as part of her formal education.

As we continued, I asked Chloe questions about each line—and even specific words—in her resume to help her prepare for an upcoming interview. We focused on how the start and end dates were described as well as her specific role and project contributions, ensuring that any results or leadership roles she had were clearly described. After all, if you only have 30 minutes to speak with someone, you want that time to be focused on content. Your resume has the power to open doors for you, so it's well worth the time to clarify all the nuances.

BUILDING YOUR RESUME

If you want to build and strengthen a resume, look for ways to demonstrate that you have developed an interest in working in healthcare and that you are taking action to prepare yourself. You might:

- Volunteer at a local hospital
- Join student groups focused on healthcare initiatives
- For spring break, work with a local community group or join a travel program through your school to learn about global healthcare needs
- Review the upcoming courses required for your major and the possible electives and adding more science- or healthcare-oriented classes

- Search for internship opportunities at companies that will provide you with more exposure to healthcare
- Take entrance exam(s) for graduate school and list the test date and results

You will know that your resume is "perfect," or at least close to perfect, when you show your resume to others and you no longer find yourself explaining nuances around the timing, descriptions, or sequence of events in your resume, and you are spending more time focused on discussing the opportunity itself and your experience for the position.

COVER LETTERS

You can communicate to the recruiter and hiring manager that you are interested in a job posting by writing a cover letter. Use these components to communicate your interest in a streamlined and effective manner:

(1) *Opening*: Introduce yourself, the college or university you are currently attending, and your academic level. Explain whether you are available to work full-time or as an intern. If you learned of this position through an event or someone who works at the company, you may include this in the opening as well.
(2) *Reference to the position*: Indicate the position you are applying for and the reason for your interest in the position and organization.
(3) *Explain your skills or interest*: Communicate how your skills and experience make you a strong candidate for the position. Identify and briefly describe any experience that may not be obvious or included on your resume.
(4) *Closing*: Express appreciation for the time that the recipient has taken to review your application.

The requirement for a cover letter varies depending on the position, and often the application will indicate whether a cover letter is required or optional. For positions that require post-graduate training such as medical school or a graduate degree (master's degree or doctorate), cover letters are often required. Having a template ready for your cover letters will make the application process easier. It is ultimately a way to connect with the hiring contacts and it allows you to add a personal touch to the application process. When writing a cover letter, pay close attention to your grammar and writing skills, as these will be assessed in addition to your other attributes.

Chloe was getting ready to apply for a position that seemed very interesting to her; however, she didn't have time to work on the cover letter. Rather than delay submitting her application, since a cover letter was not required, she simply submitted her resume. That was enough to get her application process started.

> Job postings are open for just a finite period of time, so apply as soon as possible when you see a position of interest to you.

SOCIAL MEDIA

As you are revising your resume, consider also updating your formal and informal online profiles, including your LinkedIn profile. The personal summary statement at the beginning of your profile is your online "elevator speech." What would you tell someone about yourself if you had just one minute on an elevator with their undivided attention?

In this professional summary statement, you may choose to include your major and academic studies, your personal attributes, and your professional and career interests. Presenting yourself in an authentic manner, and in a way that is consistent with your resume and cover letter, is important. Though the descriptions of your work may resemble your resume, it is not intended to be an identical match, and you may choose to list only certain details in an online profile so that it is succinct.

INTERVIEWS

It had been years since Chloe had formally interviewed for a position, since most of her internships were through professors and contacts from previous internships. She said that she definitely wanted to practice interviewing. To prepare, we chose one of the job descriptions that represented her interests and reviewed the description line by line. Chloe thought she had very few of the qualifications for the position, but I suggested that she simply start with the education requirements. Chloe could confidently discuss the technical aspects of the job, but she had to think outside the box to address the marketing and sales experience, including interacting with customers. She hadn't taken any marketing or business classes in school, but she had worked in the school's language department for four years as an office assistant, greeting guests and students and directing them to the right office. She answered the phone, made copies, and did all sorts of administrative work. This work demonstrated her interest and skills in interacting with people. Since this was not linked to her major, she originally did not have this on her resume since it did not fit "the profile" of a biomedical engineering major. After our discussion, we agreed that it did not need to be on the resume; however, she could mention this experience in her cover letter, if the position involved customer interactions or use her work in this position to share relevant examples during an interview.

Another item in the job description was "Excellent time management and organization skills, meeting deadlines." Chloe felt very comfortable with this requirement since she had established processes for managing her homework and had used them during her internships as well.

Thus, as we were preparing for interview questions, reviewing the job description relative to the experience on her resume, more examples came to mind that could be relevant for the interview. For example, working with teams and handling difficult situations were in the job description. Chloe had encountered many of these situations during her class projects and even during her internships. If there were items she did not know how to do, she wasn't concerned about it because, with each internship assignment, she had stepped into new situations, and knew how to learn on the job and teach herself new things. We continued to go through a series of questions related to the job description, and although they were thought-provoking, I noticed Chloe became calmer with each passing question, and her responses became more spontaneous.

The best way to approach interviews is to be at ease. Realize that the interviewer is asking you questions to get to know you by understanding what you have previously done and what you are capable of doing in the future. They would like to understand how you handle situations that people in their place of work (or school) encounter, and they would like to know that you have the ability to handle these or ask for guidance when needed. The expectation is not to be perfect in all areas, but still to be able to articulate your values and commitment to meeting objectives. Though a work environment with open-ended projects may seem different from school, it is reasonable to share examples from how you have handled your academic responsibilities.

Some questions are related to the work and work situations, and you want to be prepared to answer how you have handled these situations in the past and how you might handle them in a new environment. Sometimes there are online employment personality assessment tests to assess how you might interact with others and handle different situations. To prepare for these, take practice tests to familiarize yourself with the nature of the questions. If you are in a STEM major and pursuing a job related to the STEM area, you may also be presented with case studies or technical scenarios to assess your critical thinking and problem-solving skills.

For general questions, take advantage of opportunities to have "mock interviews." These are practice interview sessions that volunteers from companies or organizations offer to participate in so that students have a chance to get comfortable responding to the types of questions they may be asked.

The basic questions, which are sometimes awkward to start with, are some of the opening questions which will be familiar to you from the 5Ws in Chapter 1.

BASIC INTERVIEW QUESTIONS

- Who told you/How did you learn about his opportunity?
- Why are you interested in working here?
- Where have you previously worked?
- What experience do you have in _____? or What have you been doing since you graduated?
- When would you be available to start?

PREPARING FOR ASSESSMENT TESTS

There are several approaches I suggest as ways to prepare for assessment tests. The first is to practice taking these tests online, just like when you prepared for the ACT or SAT exams. Getting familiar with the type of questions and the pace at which you need to respond is a good way to prepare. Secondly, for personality assessments, prepare by thinking back to various situations you have been in that involved interacting with others. When were you helpful, and feel good about how you handled the interaction? When did you reflect back and wish you might have handled the situation differently? Take note of both scenarios as examples of how you might respond to situations, keep in mind your best self and how you might ordinarily handle situations. And lastly, it is best to think of these tests as just one data point among several that a hiring manager might use to evaluate whether you are a strong candidate for the position. There isn't necessarily a right or wrong answer and so you just need to be yourself and not try to second guess what the right answer should be. After all, if you want to be your authentic self in the workplace, the assessment test can go both ways in determining if an opportunity is the right match for you.

PREPARING FOR INTERVIEWS

Interviews may be conducted in person, by phone, or virtually. Whether being interviewed in person or via virtual technology, maintain a professional presence. When meeting virtually, ensure your background is simple and appropriate and your internet connectivity during the meeting is stable.

1. Learn about the company, the position, and the person you will be speaking with—for example, their title—and any information that is publicly available.
2. Be prepared to talk about your experience and share examples about the work you have done, especially experience and work related to the job description. Most importantly, build rapport with your interviewer(s) and know that during the interview, their goal is to

learn more about you and how you might be able to work with others in their company or organization.
3. Take note of the questions you are asked, and keep in mind those you might have hesitated on a response. Think of what you said, and in retrospect, what you could have said instead. Remember what you could have said so you can use it the next time that question comes up.
4. Interview preparation is important. Set aside time to practice with someone who can ask you meaningful questions.
5. Send a thank-you note after the interview; interviewers always appreciate this personal touch. Send a hand-written note within 24 hours or send an email if that will arrive faster.

Chloe was now beginning to understand how all of her experiences would come together to prepare her for her future work.

She explained:

> When I first looked at the list of descriptions, they wanted all of this specific stuff, and I don't even know if I had all the specific examples, but now that we have talked through it, I can find examples even in things that I am experiencing outside of the classroom. Previously, I had not given any value to activities beyond my educational realm, i.e., doing yardwork one summer or working retail. To be able to combine skills developed from my other experiences along with my coursework and internships for a specific job (application) has been very helpful for me.

As you are preparing for interviews, also be prepared to react to and respond to questions related to a potential offer. Even though you are just interviewing for a position, it is not unreasonable for you to be asked questions pertaining to your availability to start (start date) and salary expectations, and if pertinent, you may be asked if you are open to relocation.

INFORMATIONAL INTERVIEWS AND NETWORKING

The best time to be thinking about informational interviews and networking is before you are looking for a job or before you are making a decision about graduate school. The purpose of both of these activities is to learn more about others, so that you can reflect on what you hear and determine what resonate with you—or do not.

An informational interview is different from a formal interview (described in the Interviews section of this chapter), which is an interview after you have applied for a specific position. An informational interview is an informational discussion. The purpose is to gather information about the company or graduate program and to learn how others may have made their career decisions to work in this area. The purpose is truly informational, and not intended to be a job interview, or a request to be considered for a job.

Networking is making the effort to meet new people so that you can learn about people in a career you might be interested in. You ask people about their career journey, the companies they have worked for, and the jobs they have held. As you network, you may ask for the names and contact information for people who might be willing to meet you for an informational interview.

Informational interviews and networking can take different forms and have different names: informational interviews, networking, and building your group of "friends" and people you follow on social networks. Informational interviews and discussions are, by definition, not interviews for a job; however, they are opportunities to meet with someone and learn about their work, and ask for input on your resume or the direction you are considering for your career. They are typically one-time meetings at the end of which you may receive suggestions on others to contact or tips for job postings. Though they are not formal interviews and not opportunities to ask to be considered for a specific job, they should be taken seriously since the person may consider you for future openings, or they may refer you to someone who has job openings. These informational interviews can be arranged through family, friends, alumni, and professors, or you may look for contacts yourself as well, by browsing social networks, attending networking events, and making friends through school.

When Chloe and I started talking about informational interviews, she thought that the purpose of networking was only to meet people to discuss a specific job. But in actuality, networking is about having conversations with people and it can be people you don't know or even people you know, including your classmates. Chloe agreed. She had been so busy with classes throughout the years that she had very little time to spend with friends. Though you may be tempted to focus on getting to know people who are much further ahead in their career journey than you are, your friends are equally insightful. Chloe often talks about what she learned from a senior mentor when she was a freshman, and even from her roommates. Building relationships and mutual exchange of information strengthens connections. Networking is meant to be an enjoyable approach to meeting people, learning, preparing, and connecting for future opportunities.

Chloe had originally thought that networking was only for getting a specific position, but as we talked about networking, she started to understand the bigger picture. Her contact at the career center regularly scheduled open sessions with alumni who would meet with students, and Chloe realized how much she could learn by participating in these events. Opportunities to connect with alumni are priceless. They attended the same school as you, they know your professors and the rigor of your program, and they have an interest in your success—that's why they are volunteering their time to interact with you.

Chloe spoke with several alumni, all of whom had interesting stories about the companies they worked for. In one case, the person was the company's founder. Chloe was impressed with the scope of their work and surprised to learn that they worked for companies she had never heard of. The more she learned from the alumni, the more she looked for opportunities to connect with new people: friends, family, and people they would connect her with. The list just kept growing. She is thriving in this new approach to learning what people are doing that involve engineering and design.

Often the group of students at the alumni sessions was not too large, so Chloe was often in a small group with just one or two others, having conversations with alumni who worked at companies doing work that she could see herself doing. Many schools have alumni who try to create learning opportunities for students from their alma mater, and sometimes alumni can highlight job openings students can apply for. Generally, alumni are very willing to share insights and have a conversation, so when alumni open their doors, greet them with a warm welcome.

CONVERSATION STARTERS

Some questions you can use to engage in conversation are to start by looking for common ground:

- What did you do after graduation? Did you go to graduate school or find a job?
- What are you doing now?
- How have your studies been beneficial to what you're doing now?
- What were the most useful experiences you had in school?
- Would you do anything differently knowing what you know now?
- What have you seen others do with similar experience?
- What are the technical skills required for entry-level positions in this field?
- Can you clarify something I saw in a job description?

CONVERSATION EXPANDERS

- How did you get started in this field?
- On a typical day, what do you do?
- What part of this job do you find most satisfying?
- What part of this job do you find most challenging?
- What training or education is required for this type of work?
- What personal qualities or attributes are important to being successful in this job?
- What are the opportunities for advancement in this field?
- What kind of work experience would employers look for in a job applicant?
- What kinds of opportunities are available for someone with my degree and experience?
- How can a person obtain the experience needed to be a strong candidate before they have their first job?
- How do you see jobs in this field changing in the future?
- What are the basic prerequisites for jobs in this field?

- Which professional journals and organizations would help me learn more about …?
- What do you think of the experience I have thus far in terms of entering this field?
- If you could do things all over again, would you choose the same path for yourself? Why? What would you change?
- With the information you have about my education, skills, and experience, what other fields or jobs would you suggest I research?
- Is there anyone you recommend I speak with next?

QUESTIONS FOR YOURSELF

If your interest is working in a clinical setting, these are some questions to carefully consider:

- Can I see myself in this physical environment?
- Do I have the patience to interact with patients?
- Can I handle working with bodily fluids, even with gloves and a mask?
- Can I make patient care my priority, regardless of my personal priorities?

If your interest is in doing research, ask these questions regarding the lab:

- How does this project (or other projects) receive funding?
- Who reviews your projects? When you have questions, whom can you ask?
- What is the typical lab schedule?

NETWORKING OPPORTUNITIES

Networking in its formal sense is about making contacts and building connections that are ideally mutually beneficial. The word *networking* is used most frequently to describe networking events. Chloe described feeling awkward about networking events because, as a student, she wondered what people would think of her. Would they think she was not intelligent or didn't have enough insight into the industry or even enough knowledge about general discussion topics, such as sports, movies, or national or global news? She saw a room full of "adults" while she was just a student. It was difficult for her to randomly approach people and start talking to them. What Chloe didn't know was that many people feel uncomfortable in networking situations. However, Chloe found it easier to connect in virtual networking situations.

Networking opportunities are an incredibly valuable opportunity to learn. There are many potential benefits to attending them:

- If representatives from companies and organizations are there, you can meet them and ask questions about their company/organization and their work.
- People you meet can direct you to other resources that will be helpful to you.
- You get to practice interviewing. Even though these are not formal interviews, the conversations are like dry runs for meeting new people, introducing yourself, and telling your story. The more events you go to, the easier it gets to interact with people you have never met before.
- Remember that your presence indicates that you are interested. After all, you took the time to show up. That reflects well on you if you have an interest in that organization or meeting the individuals at a networking event.
- You will get a feel for what works and what doesn't work.

In addition, consider these pointers about networking:

- Invitations to networking opportunities may be sent to you by email or posted online. Even though the invitation may not have your name on it, if you receive it or see it and it sounds interesting, go for it!
- When you first join the meeting, or walk into the room, don't be surprised if you experience a brief moment of awkwardness. The best way to quickly overcome it is to start a conversation. Say hello to someone and introduce yourself.

- Know that the people who are at the event are there for you. They have taken time out of their schedule to be available to you and answer questions, so be prepared and ask them about questions that are on your mind.
- Questions that are reasonable to ask may pertain to your qualifications. You can ask about possible opportunities for someone with your education and experience. Having a copy of your resume on hand is recommended.
- During a networking event, you will also meet peers and you may learn from each other and even make new friends.
- At most networking events, you should wear business or business casual attire. Wear a nice outfit that fits you, in all aspects. The clothing and shoes you select should fit right—not too tight or too loose, and you should be able to move comfortably. Select colors that are flattering on you. If you don't feel that you look good in green, don't wear green. Wear something that stands out—not something loud but something noticeable because it helps people remember you. You might choose a shirt, necklace, or tie that is memorable.

Even though networking opportunities are extremely beneficial, it can be difficult to set aside the time for them. Chloe didn't like going to networking events unless a friend went with her. Meeting people she didn't know intimidated her. Granted, some were easier to speak with than others, but the idea of having one-on-one conversations with professionals just felt awkward.

You can think of these opportunities as if you are speaking with distant relatives at a family gathering. They are going to ask you basic questions about your major, your career, and your interests just to get the conversation started. Then guess what, you can take the lead from there and ask them questions about the company they are representing, their careers, or anything else related to careers that you may have an interest in.

Challenge yourself to find ways to help yourself overcome the tug to stay in and avoid these situations. One way that works for me is to focus on my curiosity about the event logistics. I always enjoy seeing how and where the food and displays are set up. So, I tell myself that while I am there, I also I get to meet people. What a great reason to step out of my comfort zone and make an extra effort to connect!

FINDING MENTORS

As you start your career journey, get to know the people you meet and build relationships with them. You will have many questions along your journey. Know who you can go to or count on when you have questions or need help. It may be one person or several people. You may have different "go to" people for different questions. These individuals may be among your family or friends, your professors, or people you meet at a networking event who are willing to provide guidance. You may have one mentor or many. If you pay close attention, you can learn from everyone you meet.

There are a few people I count on for mentorship and I stay in close contact with them on a regular basis. I check in with them every few weeks, even if it's just to say hello.

—Carlos

For more consistent guidance, Carlos, a recent graduate, describes the types of mentoring relationships that work best for him. He has an exceptionally good friend from college who he stays in contact with regularly, and they have a consistently strong relationship. In fact, they do not go for more than a month without talking. Carlos has other mentors as well, including parents and professors, who back him up.

Carlos explains,

> The idea of a mentor is to have someone who is stable, and who you can consistently depend upon to bounce ideas off of, or to vent or talk to. The reality is that some people have a hard time finding a mentor, and so you just need a good support group, an actual group of people who are interrelated, who hold you accountable, rather than individual people. This network can be like your sole mentor if you want to think about it like that.

He further shares that everyone is on their own journey and path, so you don't have to look for someone to take on that strict mentorship role.

He goes on to say,

> While I think it is important to learn from others, it is too easy to take other's experiences and project them onto yourself. While I think you can learn from other's experiences, I think you should develop your own

experiences. Think critically about how it is working for *you* and how *you* like that approach. So, I think it is great to look for mentors, but I don't think you need to get stuck on needing one mentor, or any mentors at all. You just need a solid support structure. Though you may strive to find people you can relate to, you are never going to be exactly like your mentor, even though you learn things from them. You are still going to be different from your mentor.

The same advice applies to people you meet or speak with for informational discussions. Carlos says that it is important to be able to glean a lot of new information from any experience. He is always challenging himself to take something away from an experience no matter where he is, what he is doing, or whom he is listening or talking to. This attitude has always been super valuable to him. It's easy to let your mind wander when the conversation shifts to certain topics, certain classes, or certain advice, but you still have to be able to hear a person out while being able to internalize and separate your own experience from that of others. You don't want to be too easily swayed by listening to certain opinions and lose yourself. Carlos had to be very particular about this, especially when he was on his career journey and so many naysayers were telling him that he was taking the wrong approach to his career, without really understanding who he was or what he was striving to accomplish. By holding steady, managing each life and career decision carefully, he was able to progress and find the opportunity he had searched for to launch his career.

ACTION ITEMS

1. Create a file and add the following items, templates, or updated copies of your resume and a cover letter. Create drafts of each if you are just getting started. Update your LinkedIn and other social media profiles.
2. Identify two people you don't know well or have not met before and invite them for an in-person or a virtual coffee chat. Choose people who have graduated and with whom you can schedule a mock interview so you can practice interviewing. You may choose family friends or distant relatives, or you may ask your career advisor

or professors for suggestion. Let them know you are interested in a conversation to explore careers and learn more about their field of work. Ask if you may share a copy of your resume with them in advance. End the conversation by asking if you could send them a LinkedIn request—and you'll have two new connections!

> Extra: People still appreciate a hand-written note sent through post, so find some professional-looking thank-you cards and first-class stamps. Send a card to each person you meet with. After your formal interviews, you can use the same cards and stamps to send thank-you notes.

IN CLOSING

It is essential to have these tools set up and ready to go. Some of the preparation involves writing and summarizing. Other preparation involves having a mindset that is open and receptive to doing new things, meeting new people, and learning from others. Having this framework set up early in your career journey will make it easier for you to make decisions about your direction.

3

Getting to Know and Trust Yourself

I still wonder how my personality and values would best align in a career.

—*Chloe*

What I have come to realize is that there are many good jobs and good careers, and just the same, I have come to truly appreciate people who are skillful at what they do. Just because someone says "it's a good field to work in" or "these jobs pay better than others" doesn't mean it's the best fit for you. Taking the time to know yourself will help in your career journey. These insights would also enhance how you tell your story.

DOI: 10.1201/b22077-3

GETTING STARTED—SIX SQUARES PHOTO COLLAGE

Chloe was ready to send out the resume she and I had spent a lot of time working on. We had discussed her projects and summer jobs, and she had prepared for interviews, all important activities for her career search. But as we were talking through the options, it was clear that there was more for me to learn about Chloe, and also for her to learn about herself.

A large part of the power behind a resume, cover letter, and interviewing skills—and making decisions that impact your career—comes from knowing yourself and making decisions at each opportunity that allow you to honor who you are and what is important to you. "Knowing yourself" can sound like a cliché, but it is possible to translate something that is difficult to describe in words into a framework you can use for decision making.

During the discussions that Chloe and I had about her resume, cover letter, and interview preparation, I realized we had not spent much time talking about Chloe as a person. I had certainly gotten to know her; however, as she started the interview process, it would become more important for her to know herself and her preferences well. Then she could make decisions that moved her closer toward doing work and having a lifestyle that she would be happy with.

I reflected on how I made my own decision so I could help Chloe. I first thought about the future and what I might value in my personal life. I had anticipated that I would have a family, so I had to think about the amount of time I would be spending in school and the work requirements outside of school. I distinctly recall making a decision that I was willing to commit more than four years to graduate school. Because I was working in the sciences, I would be also a working parent since science is one of those fields you would not leave for an extended period, especially in the middle of a research project. At the time there was no pressing reason for me to think about family or children. Thinking seriously about the kind of family life I wanted and how I would combine a family and a career helped me know myself better, and it contributed to my confidence that I was prepared for the commitment to pursue graduate school.

Knowing that personal values are important in a career decision, I wanted to have the same conversation with Chloe—not specifically about her future intentions but simply to understand her values at this

Getting to Know and Trust Yourself • 55

point in her life. So I asked Chloe a question that I often use to get to know the people I am meeting with: if you were to create a photo collage using six words or pictures to tell someone about yourself, what would you include?

As Chloe pondered these questions, she shared what her photo collage would look like (see Figure 3.1 for Chloe's photo collage w/ 6 squares). She likes being social but with smaller groups of people. She valued time with her family, doing yoga, and taking time to enjoy the outdoors, especially going for a run when the weather is good. She also enjoyed cooking and preparing healthy meals, and she valued being a good student. Looking at this photo collage of Chloe provided a good picture of who she is, and it became a valuable frame of reference as she explored job opportunities and made choices about the options available to her.

As Chloe and I discussed what success might look like for her, we went back to her photo collage. Chloe agreed that what drew her to work in healthcare in the first place, and whatever space she will work in in the future, she will always empathize with the end user, wanting to know their specific needs and tailoring products to meet those needs. Chloe has a love of nature, which is reflected in her interest in helping others use their natural body elements to sustain living well, in as natural a way as possible.

Other people I have worked with also noted that they value their family, and strive to be a good sibling, or a good son or daughter. They have shared their personal values of honesty, integrity, and hard work. People have also listed faith as important. At some point Chloe might consider a job that required her to relocate, and just because she values family it doesn't

Social (in small groups)	Family	Yoga
Outdoors	Cooking Healthy Meals	Being a good student

FIGURE 3.1
Chloe's photo collage w/ 6 squares.

mean that she would decline such an opportunity. Knowing herself and her preferences might help her put things in perspective and evaluate the implications of the opportunity.

The images on my own six squares when I was in college are different from what they are now. In college I started by seeing a picture of myself working in a hospital, seeing patients, being in contact with blood and other body fluids, working with people who were sick, vomiting, and feverish. That picture made it clear to me that the practice of medicine was not for me. I am grateful for the frontline workers in hospitals and clinics who risk their lives and care for people when they are at their weakest and most vulnerable. In Figure 3.2 is a collection of the six squares that represent what I embrace. I am grateful that those in clinical, patient-facing roles bring their expertise and compassion to work each day to care for those in need and that they have the patience and kindness to listen. I have had the privilege of interacting with doctors and healthcare providers who are exceptional models of these behaviors.

I care about people and their health, but the way I wanted to practice my care for others was not in a clinical or hospital setting in one-on-one interactions. This is when I realized that being pre-med was not the right path for me. I decided instead that the next step for me was learning how to understand the origins of disease, and thus I pursued a PhD in biochemistry.

Making connections between the six squares and career aspirations allows you to integrate your values into your decision. It is not intended to change what your career interests are; however, it allows you to factor

Faith	Family	Health
Food & Nutrition	Exploring	Fun

FIGURE 3.2
My photo collage w/6 squares.

these into your decision in a thoughtful manner and be prepared for situations in advance.

EXPERIENTIAL LEARNING

My fundamental belief is that you learn by doing and that there are tremendous benefits to gaining hands-on experience. Having managed an internship program for many years, I can attest to the value of this experience. Experiential learning can occur in all kinds of work, including jobs, academic projects, internships, and volunteer opportunities. If the opportunity doesn't seem to exist, and you want to learn, I suggest a DIY (Do It Yourself) initiative to create the opportunity for yourself. Though all of these options involve work of some nature, there are practical aspects to each type and sometimes the practical aspects overlap. The general descriptions that follow provide some details. Each experience can help you understand and better define your 5Ws. All of these are learning opportunities, but how they are set up differs depending on the people or organizations that set them up.

- *Job*: You are hired to do certain tasks. You will learn vicariously on the job, but these jobs, perhaps over the summer or school breaks involve work that you may or may not do in the future. Examples: Working at a local restaurant, teaching at a summer camp.
- *Academic Project*: This work is part of a class project with oversight by the professor or other designated mentors. It may be done on campus or in association with another organization. It is designed to teach certain principles, typically associated with the class.
- *Internship/Co-op*: The name varies, depending on the organization and can be labeled as such depending on your school or the host organization. In either situation, the experience can be as short as four weeks or as long as six to eight months. The experience may be a paid or unpaid. Ideally, a stipend is offered to cover your expenses; however, depending on your academic guidelines, a stipend may or may not be permissible. These experiences can be formal or informal depending on the host organization. You learn about the nature of the work and the organization, while you do work related to a

project. At the end of the assignment, you are often asked to deliver a presentation on your work. Additionally, you may learn about future career opportunities.

Volunteer Opportunities: These experiences can be on campus or at a non-profit group. They are a way to gain leadership skills and augment the work that you do separate from your internships and on the job. As a volunteer, the limit of your learning and experience is what you challenge yourself to do.

DIY (Create Your Own Opportunity): If you don't have access to an opportunity you want, light up your entrepreneurial spirit and create it yourself. Develop a wealth of new skills. Think about what you know how to do or like to do and leverage this to build your experience. You might gain or expand experience in marketing, sales, and customer interaction. You might expand your financial skills. In addition to learning or building skills, a DIY opportunity can demonstrate your initiative and organizational skills. These experiences are great ways to learn and grow.

In addition to these experiential learning opportunities, those students who said "yes" to any reasonable opportunity found they could learn just as much from others as they did about themselves along the way. There are short-term and part-time jobs, including tutoring, child care services, working retail during the holiday season, you name it, and they were willing to do it. There are so many transferable skills, such as communication skills, training, and interacting with people you can develop from accepting these types of opportunities.

As you are meeting new people and gaining experience, make note of what seems interesting to you. Do you feel inspired to learn more? Do you feel a sense of excitement at the thought of working in this field? How might this fit in with your major, your interests, and your career? Are you able to connect your interests in ways that create new possibilities for you?

As you are thinking about your career options in healthcare and overall, remember there are many ways to apply your talents. Take time to think back to the jobs you had in high school and college. Did any job involve working in a hospital or healthcare setting, working with healthcare data, or interacting with customers? Did your work involve marketing, communications (verbal or written), or social media? Do you have foreign language skills that you would enjoy applying in a work environment and using to help others? These skills and interests could lend themselves to meeting unique needs in healthcare, working in positions that require special skills.

YOUR LEARNING PREFERENCE

As you prepare for your future, knowing your learning preference will enable you to determine, for example, whether a formal classroom or a learning environment that offers interactions in a team setting suits you well. This kind of learning may include hands-on techniques. Or, do you prefer to learn independently, bypassing formal programs and trusting to teach yourself what you need to learn?

Working in healthcare requires continuous learning, so you'll want to be comfortable with coursework, certifications, and training. Some people like to read. Others like to watch videos. Learning from other people in person as opposed to learning online may be a preference. When it comes to learning laboratory or other hands-on techniques, some people like to learn through repetition and writing down the details. Knowing how you learn enables you to identify ways to help you learn those things you wish to learn, build confidence, and address the gaps that keep you from pursuing your aspirations.

Sometimes we can be overly modest, and other times, we may be overly confident. In either case, if you have come thus far in your academic endeavors, it is very likely that you can learn what you need to know. As Chloe shared,

> I recall walking into a new internship assignment and I felt totally overwhelmed by how much I didn't know, but as I started to learn on the job, and let myself explore, I found that I was able to learn and I became excited about gaining new skills. I came to realize that just like with school, if I poured myself into something and devoted the amount of time needed, I could learn and then take on these new projects.

Thus, as you are looking at career options, whether job descriptions or academic programs, you may be hesitant to apply because you do not have all the experience required. On the other hand, if you know you can learn, you can take on the new challenge and forge ahead.

YOUR 5Ws

Gaining these experiences should add to your assessment of your 5Ws.

- *Who*: Did you work with people who inspired you?
- *What*: What did you enjoy most about these experiences? Were there any surprises?
- *Where*: Did the location and the experiences of your experience shed further light on your preferences? What type of environment do you see yourself working in? Are you in an office building, a hospital, a lab, a research, or manufacturing facility, or are you working remotely? Are you in an urban or rural community? Are you working in your home country or are you abroad? Do you see yourself at a large company, a start-up, or a non-for-profit?
- *When*: At what point did you realize this work is important to you? What are your long-term goals and your timeline for your career journey?
- *Why*: In which way(s) are you strengthened by your commitment to your interests—or has there been a particular situation that has profoundly affected you?

EXPERIENTIAL LEARNING AND PREFERENCES IN ACTION

Let's look at actual examples of people who are currently working in healthcare and how they leveraged experiential learning to create the foundation for their work. Examining their 5Ws responses, we don't find a particular moment or event that built their story, nor did their answers come in any particular sequence; however, over time, their experiences have added up to form the basis of who they are and the work they enjoy doing. These responses reflect a snapshot of their journey at one point in time and capture the story of what motivates them and how they decided on their careers. As they continue their careers, their 5Ws may evolve or stay the same.

5Ws of Jasmine, a Nurse Administrator
    Who: Patients

What: Cardiology
Where: Hospital
When: Since she was in middle school
Why: She has a passion for delivering patient care

5Ws of Hannah, a Physician
Who: Patients
What: Treating their illnesses
Where: Doctor's office
When: As she was finishing college
Why: She believes that this is what she's meant to do

5Ws of Otis, a Pharmacist
Who: Patients
What: Helping them with their medications
Where: Retail or hospital
When: During sophomore year in college
Why: He enjoys interacting with people and helping them

5Ws of Mina, a Research Scientist
Who: Students
What: Teaching undergraduates about research
Where: College campus
When: Decided after completing her PhD
Why: She wants to inspire future generations

5Ws of Gabrielle, an MRI Technologist
Who: Patients
What: MRI imaging
Where: Hospitals
When: During high school
Why: It allows her to work in healthcare without pursuing a four-year degree

> I want to work in healthcare, applying my skills in biomedical engineering, design, and work with people. (Chloe)

When Chloe was in high school, her chemistry teacher noticed she was good at math and science. She encouraged Chloe to pursue a STEM career path and invited her to attend engineering workshops. When Chloe learned about biomedical engineering, it was love at first sight, and she decided this would be her major.

Chloe was fascinated that new products could be created to help doctors with their surgical procedures. As she progressed through multiple engineering classes, and especially as she added classes in design, she noticed more ways she could apply her experience than she ever would have imagined. This sparked a new passion to learn more about how she could integrate her skills into a position that would allow her to follow her interests while she defined what success would look like on her own terms.

When graduation approached, Chloe started to feel anxious about not only her exams but also her plans for the future. People had many questions for her. Would she attend graduate school? Find a job? Join the Peace Corps? She wanted to dart into a hole every time she sensed the questions approaching. She dreaded these questions, because she didn't really have an answer.

Though Chloe was feeling anxious, as a senior in college, she was also not particularly worried. She knew she had plenty of time to think about her career. After all, her grades reflected her hard work throughout her school years. Plus, her resume showcased her meaningful internship experiences. She never thought that thinking ahead about next steps should be too difficult.

Chloe constantly told herself that she just needed to find a job that was at least remotely interesting. Months earlier, Chloe had made one firm decision—she did not want to attend graduate school, at least not right after her undergraduate studies. At this point, Chloe and her classmates had been in school for about 16 years. She couldn't bear to sit in another classroom. Instead, she knew she wanted to contribute to society in a different way, one in which she could utilize her education and accomplishments from over the last four years.

Chloe knew that she wanted to work in healthcare, and she knew that she would like something different from the ordinary, but she was not certain of where to look or how to explain to others what she was looking for. She applied for a number of positions at organizations that work on healthcare products and technology. At this point, Chloe and I had one overarching goal: she needed to be able to strengthen how she communicated her story.

Though Chloe had not started to dig in yet, she had been looking into career options, and these questions made her start to wonder what motivated her, and what the right opportunity for her would look like. She acknowledged there was not necessarily a right or a wrong answer, and she knew her 5Ws would evolve over time. As a college senior, these were her 5Ws:

Who: Inspired by a manager from a summer internship
What: Open, currently meeting people and learning more about the options
Where: Open, willing to relocate, small to mid-size organization
When: Decided on major in high school and current focus while in college
Why: Wants to apply technical and people skills to product design

RESOURCE FOR CAREER INFORMATION

The *Occupational Outlook Handbook* (https://www.bls.gov/ooh/) provides a very clear and general picture of the job requirements for a wide range of jobs in healthcare and many other fields. To find this information, choose the tab "What They Do." These descriptions offer a preview of what a job posting might look like. Reviewing these descriptions and understanding the nature of the work is like taking a pre-test to check the fit between yourself (your 5Ws) and the career area you have selected and are preparing for. It can help you determine if you really want to commit your academic studies to that type of career.

You can also preview the job ahead of you by job shadowing or by doing an internship. Interestingly, sometimes seeing someone do the work is not the same as being in the job and doing the work yourself for five days a week, 10–12 hours a day. Try to imagine something so interesting that you would be willing to make this type of commitment to it. What are the speed bumps you are willing to drive over to do this work? These speed bumps could be any class or activity that is part of the job. Would you avoid this road and find a new one? Would you watch how others get over this speed bump? Look for alternate routes? Or brace yourself and give it a try? You just might be able to do it if you give it a try or ask for some help.

We all have fears and acknowledging them is part of getting to know ourselves and then being able to address them. If I were working in a hospital, would I catch every cough, cold, and flu I am exposed to? Could I draw blood from someone? Would I have the empathy and compassion necessary to help a family when a loved one is dying or in pain? My answer to these questions at the time was "no," so I needed to redirect my journey to find the opportunities and challenges where my answer to the difficult questions was "yes." What kind of commitment does the career you aspire to need from you, and are you prepared to do the work required to be good at it?

SELF-ASSESSMENTS

Another tool that Chloe used to learn more about herself was Gallop's StrengthFinders 2.0 also referred to as CliftonStrengths. This survey provides you with insights on your natural strengths that enhance your capabilities in your work and interactions with others. Chloe had not previously taken this assessment, but she knew that her roommate had, so she was curious about what it might say her strengths were. Depending on the report you request, you might receive your top five strengths or you may receive a list of all 34 in order of your strengths. As we reviewed Chloe's top five preferences, it was comforting to know that the results validated some of what she had identified as her preferences for a work environment and her style of interacting with people.

Having a report that explained her personal preferences was quite helpful as she was preparing her cover letter and getting ready for interviews. For example, if she were asked to talk about her interpersonal style or how she might handle a difficult situation, she knew that she could reflect on her strengths to reaffirm what she knew to be true. She also had language from the report and words that she could use to articulate how she approached situations.

With one of her strengths as Harmony, it seemed to reflect Chloe's preference for working in small high-functioning teams. She much preferred working in environments where she could provide input and her voice was heard. As she looked at her resume, she realized that when she was in a much larger organization, there were times when she felt lost in what was being done, and not particularly significant. Working on a smaller team—largely herself and the main engineer—made Chloe feel more important and influential and that her input mattered. Chloe valued being able to work directly with people and accomplish a goal together, and these personal preferences were reflected in her StrengthFinders report. The StrengthFinders results and work/internship experience during college may provide insights about the type of environment, culture, and interactions you prefer in a future work environment.

During the interview process, applicants are often asked questions around areas for development or improvement or things they would like to learn, and thus, if you are aware of attributes that rank lower in a list of your strengths, you may be able to share these attributes in a way that reflects awareness of yourself. Low-ranking attributes don't imply that you are not performing well in those areas; these attributes are relative to each other and not an absolute ranking of good or bad performance. With an understanding of Chloe's top five preferences, we have been able to have good conversations about how each potential opportunity fits her interests.

There are other ways to learn about yourself, including the Enneagram Personality Test, the Myers-Briggs Personality Indicator, and the DiSC Profile. I have taken each of these assessment tests over the course of my career and with each set of results, I gained more insight about myself and how I am motivated to work with and interact with others. I learned how I am internally driven and the situations that empower me. The results also highlighted some gaps, areas that I could improve upon to achieve greater results. On the positive side, the results from any of these assessments strengthen what you may intuitively sense about yourself; however, seeing it in writing helps you understand how your preferences are reflected in your career choices. When Chloe saw her StrengthFinders 2.0 report, it made a lot of sense to her that she enjoyed working in smaller organizations, and with Empathy and Connectedness also among her top five, it is understandable that she would seek customer-facing positions.

When Chloe first took the test, she wondered how the very simple and straightforward questions that seemed surface level could identify different characteristics, but they did and they did so quite accurately. She and her roommate who had taken the StrengthFinders assessment found that they had three or four of the same characteristics in their top five, so it was no wonder that they got along very well. They're both very people oriented and care about close connections.

LEARNING ABOUT YOURSELF THROUGH CONVERSATION WITH OTHERS

Chloe and I got to know each other through a class assignment for which she had to interview someone and ask about their career path. Since none of her family members work in healthcare, a friend suggested that she speak with me. Chloe remembered that I had worked in healthcare for many years, and she knew that in recent years, I was on sabbatical. I started by sharing with Chloe some of the basics, my educational background, my decision to go to graduate school, and my career in the healthcare industry.

In addition to my industry experience, Chloe was interested in hearing about my sabbatical as well. I could tell by the amazement in her eyes that she looked forward to the many things she would learn after graduation. Perhaps my conversation with her was a reminder that there is so much to learn and explore beyond the undergraduate classroom experience.

As Chloe and I continued our discussions, she started to realize that over time, she had an underlying feeling that she wanted more for herself even though she was very comfortable with her resume and the work experiences she had through college. Though she had a potential job offer, she was hesitant about the opportunity. She felt as if there was more that she wanted, and more she could do in her career. It wasn't about "settling," but about finding where she could go and what she could do that fully aligned with her personality and values.

In the beginning, Chloe started her journey with a question about how she could apply her degree without following the traditional path of going to graduate school or working in a hospital. She felt quite frustrated and even sad that she could not find the type of jobs that she was looking for, jobs that she imagined she could do.

Then, as we reviewed her resume, line by line, we came to a certificate she had listed under training. It appeared to be technical in nature, so it seemed fit to list this certificate under training; however, when I asked Chloe to explain what the certificate was for, she started to minimize it, saying that she had just taken a few extra classes. She explained that whenever people looked at her resume, they often glossed over the certificate because they did not know what it represented, so Chloe was tempted to remove it from her resume.

Well this was a signal that we should take a closer look. As we did, it became apparent that the certificate represented the design coursework she had completed. The certificate was established for students to get exposure to design, and it was a program exclusive to her school. Chloe remembered that she had made an effort to fit extra classes into her schedule so that she could earn this certificate. Then, Chloe had an epiphany. The answer was right in front of her on her resume. Over the course of her studies, she had become interested in human-centered design and had hoped that she could combine this interest with her engineering background and interact with people and patients in the development of new products.

In our ongoing discussions we had identified a cluster of words, but we hadn't been able to put it together in a coherent way until the importance of the certificate came to light. Chloe had worked hard to earn this certificate; however, to those outside of her academic community, a certificate in design had no immediate relevance. Now, though, Chloe is able to tell a very coherent story about her academic training and experiences, with all of the work she has done to get to where she is today. But the certificate that Chloe originally did not think much about became a central part of her career conversation. Now she mentions the certificate in her cover letter and explains why she is interested in the work that she wants to do. In the midst of a hectic school and work schedule, the value of obtaining this certificate was almost forgotten.

As Chloe and I sorted through positions she liked or didn't like, I remembered that she had told me that she did not like doing research. She had worked in a research lab one summer because one of her professors recommended it, so she thought that she would at least give it a try. After all, the professor said that he could see her doing well in graduate school. Although she learned a lot and enjoyed the experience, she confirmed (for herself) that research was not a career path for her to pursue.

As Chloe went back to looking at job postings, she started to see some that appealed to her. Just as completing assessment tools provides insight into yourself, looking at a wide range of job postings and gauging your reactions to them allows you to recognize what seems interesting, whether it is the specific position or the company itself. Because position titles may not always capture the full essence of the position, take time to read the entire description. Chloe had originally noticed a position that was titled product development. When she read the description, she discovered that the requirements were flexible and she met the qualifications. The description included connecting with people and focusing on the user experience, such as customer interviews and trends. The description prompted Chloe to go to the company's website, and it was not at all what she expected. Chloe liked that the job was user centered and the atmosphere seemed intriguing. Although the business developed products, they were looking for someone to oversee events! If Chloe had read only the position title, she would have missed this opportunity.

As we reviewed a list of other job opportunities, I highlighted a job that was more technical than the ones Chloe had been looking at and suggested it might be a good fit for her. In a drab, flat tone of voice, Chloe said, "Yeah that sounds interesting." But I could tell by her voice and demeanor it was not at all appealing to her. If you catch your voice saying "yes" but your body and your mind saying "no," try to understand which aspects of the situation or job you might like, and the particulars you don't like. That's okay, it's part of being honest with yourself!

Instead of disregarding an opportunity completely, reflect upon your response to become more aware of your preferences.

When you understand your preferences and the right job opportunity comes up, you are ready to pursue it because you are not going through the self-discovery and self-assessment phase while you are interviewing. You can speak with confidence about your interest and readiness for the position.

LEARNING FROM THE PAST

Chloe realized she wanted to have more conversations with people who have similar academic backgrounds to learn about options and to see how they have directed their careers. Chloe could also have had conversations with her family. Learning what her family and ancestors did may shed some light on the talents that she has, whether she is aware of them or they are hidden talents.

MAKING TIME TO LISTEN

Chloe described attending a presentation that was definitely worthwhile. The speaker was a recent graduate of the program Chloe was in. She had started her own company designing innovative healthcare products for children with diabetes. At the time of the presentation, her company was working on a new line of products for children with food allergies. Chloe was not aware such products existed, and she was intrigued to learn more about them. It gave Chloe a good feeling to know companies were doing work she is interested in.

At times in college I heard different terms and ideas that seemed interesting and learned about classes that other students were taking, and they caused me to pause and wonder. At the time, I was too busy doing what I wanted to do, so I did not take time to explore them. Now I'm taking this opportunity to suggest that when you see or hear something that causes you to pause, follow up on it. Ask questions, listen to what people tell you, and assess how any new ideas may or may not fit into your life. Someone may share a story about how they "looked into something that happened to cross their path," and it worked out well for them. Just slow down the process to listen and ask questions.

NOT MY FAVORITE SUBJECT

I wish I would have had a better understanding of my learning preference when I was in college because learning in a way that is challenging can be like having a speed bump in the middle of the road. Physics was my nemesis, but I got through it. The class that I feared the most and never even wanted to approach was Anatomy and Physiology. I have no reasonable explanation for my overwhelming, and perhaps even unwarranted, fear of this subject. I never really tried. I simply assumed I would never be able to memorize or recite all the terms. This could have been my underlying fear about going to medical school. I didn't want to do it. I didn't know how to do it. And I would do anything to self-sabotage my chances of ever getting near this subject. Well, there it is, I have shared the truth. This speed bump didn't just cause me to slow down; it stopped me in my tracks.

All of us face these proverbial, yet very real, speed bumps in our life and career, and just like the physical speed bumps in the roads, they have a purpose. Physical speed bumps are near schools, hospitals, and other places where driving fast could endanger your safety and the safety of others. Proverbial speed bumps make us slow down a little or even stop because we need to think about what we are doing.

Knowing yourself means you can sense what your speed bumps might be. They are subjects you don't like, work you don't really want to do, and the things you fear might cause you embarrassment if anyone knew your feelings about them. I can assure you that when I was in college, I never told anyone that I was afraid of the need to learn anatomy and physiology. I never gave anyone a chance to help me and I never even asked how others did it. I simply did not want to get near this speed bump. Understand that with a strong sense of self-confidence I had the courage to drive over other speed bumps preparing for life and career—just not this one.

If I were to try to tackle anatomy and physiology today, I would probably make it more fun. I would start with a coloring book and nice markers. Then I would find some tools online that would make it easier for me to learn from. I would also add in some self-rewards as incentives for progress!

Every career journey has speed bumps, and many of the decisions you make will likely have elements that you would simply prefer to avoid. Perhaps you know what they are, or perhaps you need more time to think about them. Taking time to learn and plan how you will address these speed bumps may save you from feeling frustrated and disappointed along your journey.

Even though some decisions are very planful, there are times when you just need to trust your gut, follow your heart, and say "yes" to opportunities that present themselves to you. Ask others ... many will share that this is how their careers started. They were inquisitive and open and took steps that felt like the "right thing to do" as well.

*—**Leon***

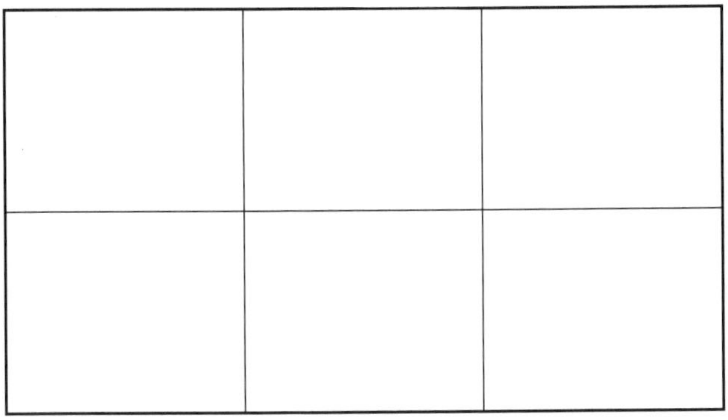

Getting to Know and Trust Yourself • 71

FIGURE 3.3
Create your photo collage w/6 squares.

ACTION ITEMS

1. Create a photo collage of six keywords or photos that are important to you. (See Figure 3.3 for your template.)
2. Is there a topic or subject matter that is your nemesis and that you really would like to overcome? Try finding a friend who is good at it and brainstorm ways you can learn and improve.

IN CLOSING

Knowing yourself will help you build a strong connection with your work and livelihood that will motivate you to endure and succeed. Taking the time to explore and learn from others and having an understanding of this foundation is the gift you give yourself on this journey.

4

Becoming Comfortable with Uncertainty

To grow, you sometimes have to be prepared to stand on ground that is always shifting a bit, moving. But you are trending upwards, looking for a way to step up to better opportunities.

—Carlos

Being honest and knowing my personal and professional preferences has been the best approach for me to follow throughout my career journey. I will admit, though, that there were many times I wished that someone knew me well enough to tell me exactly what to do and which direction to take. That never happened. Only I would know what I needed to do to remain true to myself.

Even when I trusted that I was headed in the right direction, I had a keen sense of awareness that as I stepped out of my comfort zone, managing uncertainty would be an inherent part of the process. Leveraging my 5Ws as a guide allowed me to step forward with confidence despite uncertainties that lay ahead.

Uncertainty can take several forms. There is the uncertainty of the world around us. There is the uncertainty about decisions that other people make that impact our lives. There is also the uncertainty within ourselves and our decisions. Though you can never have all the answers and know where each decision about your journey will lead, it is important to trust yourself and to trust that you are headed in the right direction. I have found that being more comfortable with uncertainty and holding myself accountable where I could, made handling uncertainty more manageable.

ACCEPTING UNCERTAINTY

As a sophomore in college, I was coasting through my chemistry classes. I particularly enjoyed organic chemistry. One afternoon, I was in the lab doing an experiment as part of the lab class and the experiment called for a distillation. I had made a mistake and overlooked a step, so I tried to add back one solution that was hot, to another solution that was cold. That was a bad idea.

I was paying attention, and before I could even scream, I noticed a small burst of flames where embers had landed on my sweatshirt. It was one of my favorite sweatshirts that sported Mickey Mouse. I quickly patted down the flames to save Mickey, obviously, because I could not lose this sweatshirt. The teacher's assistant ran to me with a fire extinguisher. Fortunately, 911 did not have to be called, and my sweatshirt didn't make the campus news.

From that day forward, I had to reconsider how I would apply my chemistry degree because even the thought of causing something to break out in flames was not comfortable for me. In retrospect, more training and experience might have alleviated that concern, but as a sophomore, I could only feel that working in a chemistry lab was not right for me. The thought of changing my major never crossed my mind and I continued through my junior and senior years taking all of the requirements to major in chemistry.

I didn't change my major because I liked chemistry as a subject, especially as we got into more advanced level classes when I learned about physical chemistry (PChem) and quantum theory. I also didn't know how I might apply my chemistry training, but for me, completing my bachelor's degree was a prerequisite for continuing with the next phase of my life. The best analogy I can offer is that even though I didn't know which path I wanted to take or even which mountain I wanted to climb, I was persistent about getting to the other side.

Throughout my studies and career as well as those of others I have coached, having self-sustaining strategies to guide yourself through times of uncertainty can make it easier to take small steps toward progress.

STAYING GROUNDED

I was already feeling pretty uncertain about what I wanted to do, and I still don't know what I want to do, but it has prompted me to think about how else I could apply my skills.

—*Chloe*

Whether your decision is to become a physician, a nurse practitioner, an engineer, a scientist, or a healthcare administrator, questions about your decision may come up. You may ask yourself whether you have made the right choice about any number of things. Other people may ask if you have considered other options. They may ask why you chose to pursue one career over another. Or people may say nothing at all, leaving you to wonder if you have made a good choice.

Furthermore, depending on what is happening in the world around us, policies, global needs, or industry requirements may change. As the saying goes, change is constant, and with changes often come concerns. Being aware while staying grounded will help you weather the changes and address the questions that may arise.

When I was still thinking about medical school, healthcare delivery models were expected to change. The news and various journals were full of information about these changes. As a student, I didn't have anyone to turn to with my questions about what might be the reality for physicians and the impact of these proposed changes. In an effort to have a better understanding, I recall mentioning the subject to people who worked in healthcare professions, but the response, even from seasoned professionals, was typically similar to one anticipating bad news. They would typically shrug their shoulders and gaze at the floor and with a look of dismay and concern on their faces.

In hindsight, this uncertainty and speculation around industry changes clouded my mind and made me concerned about pursuing medicine. The only way for me to stay grounded in my decision was to reflect upon my 5Ws and know that I was contemplating a change, not because of the speculation but because I wanted to be involved in research.

I have come to understand that change in any industry is inevitable. Depending on the nature of the change, new guidelines or regulations may apply, or new ways of operating may disrupt an entire industry. Ultimately, these changes may affect the cost or value of a product or service. Anyone working in an industry or occupation with major changes or disruptions on the horizon would feel challenged.

Realize that changes and business disruptions create opportunities as well. Let's say there are disciplines in science or engineering, or there are certain medical or technical professions that are viewed as less popular. Then there is a major change or disruption and then there is a need for advancements in a particular discipline or people with certain expertise.

The reverse can happen as well. There can be a lot of hype and excitement around a certain job or line of work, giving you the impression that this work is highly lucrative. But then, due to changes in the business or the economy, the number of opportunities may shrink or the need may change. The same may hold true for a field of work that seems very interesting or promising while you are in school. The field may change, and how you do your work may be reshaped or change altogether from how you anticipated doing it. In these situations, the changes are external to you. If they occur, review your 5Ws and use them as your anchor to stay grounded in what you believe you are good at and what is important to you. Then explore how you can adapt under the circumstances.

As I sought answers to my questions about how healthcare delivery might change, no one could offer any definitive insights. How could they know what was to come? Everyone was facing uncertainty and could only speculate about the potential impact.

Ultimately, I did not want circumstances beyond my control to overly influence my decision and shape my career preferences. I wanted to make a decision that allowed me to stay true to myself, while taking into consideration, and being aware of the world around me. I realized that as a new college graduate, I still had so much to learn that regardless of the decision I made, if I enjoyed doing the work, I would find a way to apply what I would learn.

To help manage the uncertainty of external influences, find people who work in this field and ask questions related to their 5Ws and include several "how" questions, such as:

- How long have you been doing this work?
- What does a good day on the job look like, and what does a bad day, a really bad day, look like?
- What keeps you committed to your job?
- What changes do you anticipate in this field over the next 3–5 years?
- How might these changes impact your work?
- What are some options a student might consider if they have an interest in this field?

As you ask these questions, view this as information gathering and not absolute. An individual's perspective is simply that. It's not right or wrong, good or bad; it is simply information from their perspective they are sharing to help you glean insights for your career and decisions.

The information they provide will hopefully help you stay grounded in your decision. These insights may address or solidify any uncertainties you have concerns about. Or they may lead you to consider other options. The key is that having perspectives from people who do this work will help you know what to expect and how to prepare for it.

Another aspect of staying grounded is holding your own, and living by your decision. When Carlos graduated from college, he wanted to take time to learn about ecommerce. He had a plan for himself. Others, especially family members, were nervous and anxious about his decision. They thought he should be looking for a full-time job. This can happen when others have never taken the path you have chosen. Or they might have seen others take what appeared to be the same path, and the results did not seem favorable.

I have had the same experience. In fact, there were several important career moves I made that I was challenged on. The first of these was when I made the decision to go directly from graduate school into a job in the healthcare industry. My family was pleased that I had a good career opportunity; however, this career move was not well-received by the faculty in my graduate program. It was very clear that they had hoped that I would stay in academia but I chose to stay grounded in my decision. Another example is when I moved from a technical role into a position in human resources. This time, it was my family who expressed concern about my career move, since I had invested so much time earning my PhD.

In both situations, the "what" part of my 5Ws had evolved. When I moved from research in academia to research in industry, I wanted to understand how science done on a benchtop was developed and delivered into the hands of a patient or customer. When I moved from research and development into human resources, I wanted to understand how to impact the business through leadership and talent development. I was eager to accept these opportunities, but I was a bit nervous as well. After all, I had been working in a lab for most of my career. Holding steady and being comfortable accepting that I was heading into new territory kept me grounded.

I know I would be ready to move and relocate for the right job opportunity.
—Chloe

BEING PREPARED

Though there may be uncertainty in circumstances beyond your control, your commitment to yourself and being emotionally prepared can help you manage some aspects of the unknown.

Before I completed my undergraduate degree, I had made the decision to go to graduate school. At the time, I didn't know exactly where I was going or what type of program I would enroll in, but I knew that I was going to make a personal commitment to continuing my education. And also, I decided I would plan to go to graduate school right after college and not postpone this until later. I have since known many people who go back to school at different times in their lives. They enroll in MBA programs, medical school, master's degrees, teaching certificates, and many other degrees long after completing their undergraduate studies. For me, it was the right decision to continue my studies directly after graduate school. There was so much more I felt that I needed to learn.

I also made a commitment to myself that I would be a working parent throughout my career. Thus, I anticipated that in the future I would learn to manage both career and family. This held true. I felt better prepared to handle both family and work life, in part, because I made a personal commitment to both very early in my career.

As I have interacted with students and professionals over the years, I have seen geographic location shape and influence career decisions as well. Whether your next step is continuing your education or finding a full-time job, the geographic location can be a key determining factor. For some people, the geographic location is a top priority. For others, the priority is the best opportunity regardless of the location. You may find yourself considering a move to another part of the country, or even to another country altogether.

When considering a need to relocate, some of the topics I have suggested students consider are practical aspects:

- Friends and family
- Cost of living
- Establishing new friends and a professional network
- Variety of employment options within the region

I have had the benefit of being in a large metropolitan area that has offered, at least for my needs, the best I could hope for in terms of schools and career opportunities. I have been close to family, and a large variety of food and culture is easily accessible. Thus, for many reasons, I have not had to face the decision of making a geographical move. But I have assisted many people with relocations, and the change is often welcome. It ultimately becomes both a personal and professional decision.

DAY-TO-DAY UNCERTAINTY IN HEALTHCARE AND RESEARCH

Mina, a research scientist who is working in a post-doc position, describes healthcare and science and the importance of being comfortable with uncertainty. She explains,

> Healthcare, to me, vacillates from the known to the unknown. Sometimes, the questions are easily answered. This is a wart. That is a cold. This is food poisoning. But other times … we don't know why a person is sick. "How can we make them feel better?" "What can we do to keep them alive?" "What are things we can offer to make their lives just a little easier?" The science of healthcare involves living in the unknown, so that we can bring what is known to light, and help people live, be healthy, or even survive. I must say that I didn't realize that going through graduate school, talking about being uncomfortable, I never knew if [answers to the] questions I had were not known to the world, or simply something I didn't know.

Mina continues to elaborate.

> Imagine going through life that way. All around the world, researchers are looking for answers. Millions of dollars of grant money are used to fund research because there are so many questions that we need to answer. We're generating new data and we're trying to interpret that data. Remember the bigger picture. You are not alone when dealing with uncertainty, especially for those doing clinical research.

This is the core of scientific advancements, thus being comfortable with the uncertainty associated with research is vital.

DOING THE WORK

Sometime people think that becoming a doctor is out of reach for them, but it's not. You don't have to be a rocket scientist. You just have to be willing to do the work and be good at what you choose to do.

—Leon

Becoming Comfortable with Uncertainty • 81

Growing up, I was responsible for taking my grandparents to the doctor's office since they couldn't speak English. I enjoyed speaking with the doctors, so much so that I learned clinical terms, medical instructions, and more from an early age. The doctors I encountered always had such a pleasant way of interacting with their patients. I could see myself in their shoes. A career in medicine seemed like the right choice for me. Although I was exposed to numerous career options as a teenager, my favorite interactions always happened in doctor's offices. I became passionate about learning how to help others heal.

However, as my grandmother aged, friendly doctor's visits turned into urgent care needs and visits to the emergency room. There, I saw the brevity of human life once again. This took me back to my childhood, and flashbacks of seeing my mother in her last days, and it left me feeling overwhelmingly sad. I started to wonder if I could truly put my heart and my soul into interactions with patients on a daily basis working in a clinic or hospital setting. I was faced with the uncertainty of how to balance my interest in understanding the principles in treating ailments and disease with the actual day-to-day responsibility of medicine, helping people stay alive.

It seems obvious now, but doing the work is different from thinking about doing the work or imagining what it must be like to do the work. I have come to learn in many instances that when you have the opportunity to experience doing the work or at least have a close-up view, you learn much faster. Gaining hands-on experience through a summer job or internship may take some of the uncertainty out of the question of whether or not you might like the day-to-day responsibilities associated with a career.

Finding a volunteer or job opportunity at a healthcare clinic while I was in high school or college would have been beneficial for me. I would have learned more, not only about working in a healthcare environment but also about other healthcare opportunities I could have considered.

During college, I did have internship experience, and beginning in my freshman year I spent each summer working at a research lab in a hospital. A family friend who was a physician and researcher had helped me identify this opportunity so that I could gain an understanding of diseases from a scientific perspective. As a freshman, I had never worked in a biochemistry lab, so I was eager to accept this opportunity.

I enjoyed every aspect of my research internship. I was learning new laboratory techniques and involved in designing what might become a laboratory test to help in the diagnosis of rheumatoid arthritis. Gaining hands-on experience in the lab, analyzing the results, and having dynamic conversations about the next experiment created a rhythm that resonated with me. Each day I found myself enjoying new challenges. I would spend each summer working in this same lab throughout college. This experience in a research lab prepared me for graduate school.

I recognize that finding summer job opportunities is not always easy, especially when there are so many things you want to experience. I encourage you to take advantage of opportunities that do present themselves, especially early in your college career. Even if the opportunity itself does not seem to be an immediate fit for your interests, it is a chance to learn. One of my students was receptive to every opportunity that came up. She worked retail during the holidays, volunteered at a child care center near campus, and helped a small business with marketing through social media. Through these experiences, she gained a variety of skills and most importantly, she put herself in new and uncomfortable situations, so she learned to adapt to the uncertainty associated with learning new things and meeting new people.

TAKING ACTION

As soon as I knew that I no longer wanted to be a chemical engineer, I spoke with my Dad and we explored other options.

—Otis

What I didn't realize was that when I changed my career decision in college, I was also letting go of what had been my safety net for so many years. I had held a vision for myself and had articulated this to others. When I changed my mind, I anticipated facing the fear and embarrassment of telling people the truth. I couldn't help but wonder what people would think or say. I couldn't keep these feelings to myself, nor was I willing to pursue a career that I was no longer certain about. I decided to take action and start new conversations even though they might be considerably awkward and uncomfortable.

I knew that depending on whom I spoke with, different emotions would be stirred up while explaining my decision. Yet I realized that I was ultimately the person responsible for my decisions and how they would affect my future. All I knew at the time was that I would not be happy in a clinical setting working directly with patients.

Telling your family, friends, and others that you are changing course can be difficult. Some will be respectful and supportive of your decision. Others may challenge you or even make you feel bad or second guess your decision. Even if they don't say anything, it is a difficult phase to be in, especially when it seems like everyone has a plan except you. Hold steady, this stage doesn't last forever, especially if you take time, hold yourself accountable for figuring out what you want to do, and then prepare to take action.

As I proactively communicated my concerns and my need to look at other options for my career, this opened up opportunities for me to explore. Based on the experience I had working in a research lab, I decided to look into the requirements to enroll in a PhD graduate program. I started to perk up and pay closer attention to the science around me and the research that was happening. I became excited at the prospect of looking at graduate programs and started to reach out and visit different schools, even considering options that were far from home.

Before reaching out, some might have asked what it was like to be in a PhD program. Some might have been concerned about the uncertainty associated with the amount of time it might take to complete enough research to defend a thesis. Interestingly, once I found the path that I wanted to pursue, I gathered the enrollment information I needed from the graduate school programs, and made the personal commitment to move forward.

There were many uncertainties in the road ahead. On the one hand, some might have suggested I gather as much information as possible. I will agree that it would have been helpful. On the other hand, I didn't ask for a lot of input either because each person's journey is different. If someone told me that graduate school was great and it was easy, I knew that my experience wouldn't necessarily be the same. If someone told me it was really hard and they quit, it didn't mean that I shouldn't try or give up on my dream. I wanted the desire to come from within and not be overly influenced by others. By taking a deep breath and stepping forward, what seemed overwhelming at first became more manageable as I gained first-hand experience.

PROBLEM SOLVING

It's all about deconstructing complex problems and making them as simple as you can. Reduce difficult problems into problems you have solved before. No matter what field you are working in, it's all about problem solving, critical thinking, and understanding how to develop solutions.

—*Carlos*

Learning how to solve problems and getting a lot of practice at this builds muscle memory for handling the unknown. One doesn't need to be a research or rocket scientist to develop these skills.

Minareflects on her experience doing research as an undergrad and graduate student:

> Your project has its ups and downs. Experiments might work one day, and not the next. What is fascinating and what motivates the research scientist is that you are doing work that may lead to breakthroughs in medicine. Getting a PhD requires persistence. Advisors change. Their funding changes. They move labs. Every discovery you make may not have been previously known to mankind. Through ideas you have in your mind, using whatever techniques that are available or models that you create, you can discover something that no one else in the world knows, and you document this and submit this for peer review in a scientific journal. If it is accepted for publication, your work, your research, is published for the world to see and is in the annals of history forever. You may get to present this at an international conference where you speak with other like-minded scientists about this topic. After all, they are the people who understand every detail of what you have been working on day and night, the things that you dream about. What is scientific research? It is where vaccines and medicines come from; it is how people understand the nature of disease and aging. It is how one learns how to give the gift of life to an infant who might have otherwise not survived with a defective heart. If you like asking questions and looking for answers and engaging others who are equally passionate about these topics to work with you, this is what research is all about. Research

> can save lives. It's not for the faint of heart. It requires hard work and persistence but allows one to truly define and explore the world of nature and create solutions for humanity. This is the ultimate reward for being comfortable with uncertainty.

Conducting research is like building muscle memory. Completing experiments repeatedly and seeing different results can help you become more comfortable with the idea of not knowing, with the overall notion of uncertainty. Some experiments prove to be faulty. Other experiments prove to be beneficial. Yet others are inconclusive. By working this experimental muscle group, you'll gain persistence, faith, and understanding that the answer will come, even if it takes longer than you had initially anticipated.

Carlos reflects on lessons learned doing aerospace research as an undergraduate majoring in physics:

> Unlike my previous lab projects, this research internship was the first experience I ever had where uncertainty was a huge portion of the work. I was forced to find ways to figure things out when there was no clear answer. This undergraduate research provided me with a tangible way, early in my career, of asking questions to find what could be an answer. Regardless of where you work, you will need this skill. It is the most valuable asset that I have.
>
> Imagine the day-to-day challenges one might face working in healthcare—patients have undiagnosed symptoms; test results don't make sense; equipment may be faulty. You may be stumped as a medical professional and cannot readily identify specific problems. Your patient's health and livelihood are at stake. No matter what career you choose, the ability to address and solve problems is a highly valued skill.

Otis reflects back to when he first started his career as a retail pharmacist and shares his insights:

> If you find yourself in a brand-new situation, my best advice to you is to figure out how to solve your most basic problem and build up from

> there. The reality is that anyone you deem to be a successful individual all started where you are. In order to get to the next level in their career, they needed to solve their own problems by connecting with people who are subject matter experts (SMEs). This starts by building a network, building rapport with people, and having friends and colleagues who will pick up the phone when you call. If you feel like you don't have a network, take the time to start building one.

A willingness to embrace uncertainty has been instrumental to my ability to move across functions and take on new challenges throughout my career. Doing research has taught me to be humble, accept that I don't know everything, and that others don't have all the answers either. When we know we are not the only ones searching, it makes easier to start the conversation and ask, "I wonder what the best way to approach this is."

IT'S OKAY TO ASK

I'm not sure why, but in school, I have always had this feeling like we are all supposed to have the answer. It would be awkward to admit you didn't know something.

—Chloe

During times of uncertainty, especially when you don't have the answers, trust that someone out there might be able to help. When you start to ask questions, answers start to appear when and where you least expect to find them.

Throughout her years in college, Chloe thought that she had to figure it all out on her own. She needed to decide on her major, her internships, and even what to do after college. She wanted to make her own decisions. As she was entering the second semester of her senior year, the pressure started to build up inside her. She had worked so hard to do well, and she was surprised to suddenly find herself at a loss. She thought she had a plan and that the job she wanted would be easy to find online. After all, hundreds of jobs are posted there. Looking but not finding the jobs she wanted, or thought existed, she started to feel a sense of despair.

She was grateful for her support network, but now it wasn't enough. Fortunately, help was just a phone call away. Chloe had received emails with invitations to sign up for conversations with school alumni about their career paths. In the past, she would have been hesitant to sign up for these since they could be awkward. With an understanding of the benefits of networking, Chloe had a renewed sense of enthusiasm around opportunities to connect with and learn from alumni. She signed up for these virtual coffee chats right away. Since there were few others on the calls, she practically had one-to-one conversations with alumni. She finally had the courage to ask the question that was simmering in her mind, but that she had not previously been able to articulate. She wanted to know what types of opportunities were available for a biomedical engineering major who doesn't want the typical biomedical engineering job.

This question would have been extremely difficult, if not embarrassing, to ask in a classroom discussion in front of 20 other people, but in a one-to-one conversation, Chloe felt more at ease about asking it. The insights she received helped her realize that others have been in her situation and they found career options. This gave her the reassurance that she would find her way as well.

Sometimes you may want to ask for general career guidance. In other instances, the questions you need to ask are for very clear and definitive information. Having the right information allows you to make better decisions, or even simply allows you to do your work more responsibly. I used to think I needed to have all the answers, but that is neither true nor realistic.

Emma, a recent graduate, started a new job and shared this thought:

> As long as I humbled myself, other people are not going to expect me to know how to do something, especially if I am new in this career path. No one is going to expect you to come in and have all the answers. However, they are going to probably be very disgruntled with you if you pretend like you have all the answers or don't ask any questions. So, it's okay if you ask people who have been doing this a lot longer than you to seek out support, make it less scary, and be open to new opportunities.

Otis, who has managed a team of up to 30 pharmacists, shared this advice:

> Take time to find out the right answer since people don't expect you to have all the answers, because if you have the wrong answer, people will find out. Just say, "Let me double check and find out." There is no shame in this.

UNCERTAINTY, A PART OF BEING

In hindsight, I now recognize that for a period of time, I was so immersed in my own anxiety about wanting to find certainty amidst uncertainty that I overlooked the obvious. If I had looked at my college resume from a different perspective, as if it were not my own, my interests and the answers to my questions were right in front of me. I would have recognized that my interests after graduation would gravitate toward research and biochemistry. After all, I did research for four summers in a biochemistry lab. My decision to go to graduate school was just the first of numerous career decisions I would later make.

Being in a PhD program is wildly different from being an undergraduate student. For starters, undergrads, on average, take four years to complete their degree. They have to fulfill certain requirements to receive a degree. But graduate school is its own beast, requiring independent research with uncertain timelines. Completion is represented by a defense of your thesis in front of your graduate thesis committee.

My original project, though very interesting, involved using magnetic resonance imaging and spectroscopy to collect data from patients with tumors. The particular technology we were using was still in development. Though it was clinically very interesting research, it was not feasible for me to do novel or investigative research. Thus, my graduate thesis committee recommended that I find a new advisor and a project that was more suitable for my graduate studies.

I wanted to complete my PhD degree and so I met with several professors in the department. Ultimately, there were two projects of particular interest to me, both with potential clinical relevance. One professor was an expert in the nutritional benefits of omega-3 fatty acids in the diet. Another professor was studying mouse mammary tumor virus (MMTV). The research opportunity to study the tissue-specific regulation of mouse mammary tumor virus was the right project for me. At that time, there was no proven correlation between mouse mammary tumor virus and breast cancer in humans; however, it was suspected that we could learn from MMTV. For that reason, I signed up to work on this project. I welcomed this opportunity to learn molecular biology and the science behind retroviruses.

Over the years, students have asked me if they should consider graduate school. It's a very personal decision since it takes commitment and persistence. No one will ever tell you it is easy; however, those who have completed their degrees will tell you they are very glad they did.

I was in a good situation with my second research project, and working with my advisor, my research contributed toward the publication of two research papers where I was included as an author. What this also meant was that my thesis defense was now within reach. Soon, I would be ready to graduate, and once again, it was time again for me to think about the next steps.

COMING FULL CIRCLE

As I was completing my research and writing my PhD thesis, the same questions came up again:

- What are you doing after graduation?
- Will you be doing a postdoc?
- Will you be looking for a job?

The only response I could offer was "I don't know." There were good reasons for all of these options, but I simply did not know which route I would select, nor did I know which options would be available to me.

It is customary, though not required, for research scientists to consider doing a postdoc after graduate school, so I started to think about the type of postdoc position I would want for myself. Then, a family member forwarded an announcement for a career fair at a healthcare company and suggested I take a look at it. I was hesitant at first. There were many thoughts and questions running through my mind:

- Do I have time to be away from the lab?
- Who will I talk to?
- What will I have to say?
- How do I respond if they ask about my graduation date?
- How does my current research prepare me for a job in industry?
- Will a postdoc be required?

I could have selected any of these reasons as an excuse not to attend this recruiting event, but my family strongly encouraged me to attend. To this day, I'm extremely thankful that I decided to attend, as it ultimately resulted in a job offer and an opportunity for me to work in the healthcare industry. This life experience showed me that one decision amidst a sea of uncertainty can change your entire career trajectory. One event led to a new opportunity, one that I never would have never imagined possible if I had not accepted the invitation to give it a try.

Accepting the invitation was just the first step. Next, I needed to update my resume and be certain I had the right attire. Though it was not a formal interview, I still wanted to look professional—fashionable, but not overly trendy, a splash of color without being loud. On the day of the event, once again, I again had a lot of uncertainty.

- Where do I go?
- Am I dressed appropriately?
- Will my resume show enough experience?
- What type of position(s) are they interviewing for?

Never would I have imagined that my first job would be as a scientist at a global healthcare company. Working for a company that manufactures laboratory tests to diagnose medical diseases was just right for me. I enjoyed working with people, so leading a team and working toward a common goal was energizing for me. My first role was as a project manager, overseeing the development and launch of a new diagnostic test that was a biomarker for heart attacks. From this experience, I learned that I had to be comfortable and confident in my decisions, even when I didn't know what the future would hold for me.

As my career progressed, I moved into research and development. I experienced the importance of our work more and more each day. When our products generated a test result, they made a difference in someone's life. As my role within the company expanded to leading others, I realized the impact that people make in an organization.

FOLLOWING MY HEART

My first exposure to the function of a human resources department was during the formal training classes I had as a manager. At the end of this series of classes, the Vice President, Human Resourcescame and spoke with us about the importance of people and talent in the organization. Her message had a lasting impact on me, and I developed a newfound interest in human resources as a function. She told us that our senior leader thought about his people all the time.

Thus, when an opportunity became available for me to take a six-month assignment in Human Resources, I said yes. It was not my first time in a six-month assignment. Earlier in my career, I had a six-month assignment in marketing.

This time, my research and development project had come to a close, and I was looking for a new position. The opportunity to help scientists and engineers find new positions as part of their career transition seemed like the perfect opportunity for me to learn more about human resources. Though it was all very new for me, I welcomed this opportunity to get a different perspective of the business. What was originally a six-month assignment went on for a year and a half, and I then continued in human resources for the next 15 years of my career.

Meeting with the scientists and engineers, I would learn about their careers and aspirations. With the right experience, a research and development scientist could move into a position in the regulatory affairs department, or if they had an MBA, they might even transition into a job in marketing. In addition to my own career pivot, I gathered insights and experience to guide people through transitions from one career to another.

Though I worked in many functions within human resources, the work that I was most continuously involved in was recruiting. Over the course of time, I was responsible for candidates at all levels of the organization, from interns to executives, and across all functions: science, engineering, and clinical roles, as well as human resources, marketing, IT, and finance. We even hosted students from all over the world for internship opportunities.

These career moves were significant departures from what one might have imagined would be my career path based on my education. However, timing, attentiveness to opportunities, taking action in response to invitations, and being comfortable in times of uncertainty has allowed me to embrace new experiences.

ACTION ITEMS

Write your thoughts and journal on these two topics using the space provided or in your own private journal.

1. What are you most proud of learning on your own?
2. What career-related activity(s) would be beneficial for you to participate in?

IN CLOSING

Being comfortable with uncertainty allows you to venture into areas that are completely new to you. Acknowledging that you are taking a leap and being mentally prepared for new experiences is key. Being ready to learn, embracing the environment, and staying focused on why you made your decision (your 5Ws) keeps you grounded in your endeavors.

5

Growth: Bridging the Gaps and Continuing to Learn

Perhaps it's an academic thing, but when you are in school, whether you are with your classmates or your professors, it's hard to admit you don't know how to do something. One would be embarrassed if you said you didn't know how to do something or if you had any gaps, especially if you are known to get good grades or at the top of the class ... people have a certain impression of you.

—*Chloe*

DOI: 10.1201/b22077-5

You have been climbing mountains, one after another and yet, another one is ahead, one that you want to reach, but the path to the mountain has gaps. They are not good or bad, they are simply a natural part of the landscape. With each success comes new challenges.

Some of the gaps you might be able to anticipate because they are on the map. Most of those gaps are requirements like specific classes or a degree. Other gaps might be unplanned but still a welcome adventure. When you embrace learning as a way to grow, then you see these gaps as opportunities rather than obstacles.

When Chloe and I first started having career conversations, I shared with her that even though as a professional I had been in the work environment for more than 20 years, I was still learning. There were gaps in my life and areas for me to work on and develop. Chloe looked at me, smiled, and breathed a sigh of relief. She was reassured to know that even someone who graduated from college years ago can feel that they have gaps.

THE GAPS

Gaps are not homework assignments or things that others tell you to do. They are challenges that you come upon in your life and career journey. The name *gaps* help call your attention to and focus on areas you may want to work on. When you are numb to your gaps and work toward goals that may have changed, you may look up and find yourself in a spot that is not quite where you intended to be. There is no judgment here. It's not about whether you are good or bad at something. The gap points out what needs to happen so you can work toward the next step.

Being attentive to where you are and where you want to be allows you to take deliberate actions to close the gaps as you move along your career journey. As you approach these situations, the most important thing to do is not take immediate action. Instead take time to pause and ask yourself what would truly make you happy. The goal is that by identifying and then addressing the gaps, you make progress in the right direction. If you are happy with exactly where you are and where you are headed, you may think of these not as actions toward gaps per se but rather as actions that have a positive impact on your perspective.

Growth • 97

There are many kinds of gaps and they are created by a variety of situations. Some of the common gaps and their possible reasons include:

- You have wanted to learn skills or investigate topics, but you have not had the time.
- You have a new job or new responsibilities and you want to learn and be better at what you are asked to do.
- The job descriptions you review include academic requirements, which you have, but there are other experiences listed, only some of which you have.
- Certain situations make you uncomfortable and you avoid them if you can mostly because you don't feel like you have a strong skillset in that area.
- Opportunities to advance your career are available, but you are missing some important skills or experience.
- Gaps in the form of time, such as in between graduation and your first job.

I WOULD IF I HAD TIME

Are there classes you wish you could have fit into your schedule? Are there technical or communication skills you would like to develop? These are the gaps between what you would like to do and what you might do if you had more time.

Carlos was in his last year of college and he was finalizing his class schedule. He was looking at the list of courses and breathed a heavy sigh. He was graduating soon and there was so much more he wanted to experience. All through college, he had focused on math and science courses. His friends were business, marketing, and finance majors, and their classes sounded interesting, too. Up to this point, Carlos had not had time for classes other than requirements for his major. Carlos was planning to take several advanced-level science classes during his senior year since he had progressed to the level where he could handle the complexity.

The more he thought about the fact that this was his last semester in college, the more he started to feel unsettled about what felt like being on autopilot. It was certainly part of the natural progression for someone with his research experience to be qualified to take graduate-level classes, but was that really what he wanted? After all, he had already decided he did not want to go to graduate school.

He asked himself two simple but thought-provoking questions. What has he not had exposure to during college that would help him graduate with a well-rounded set of skills? What was he eager to learn?

Just before Carlos had to finalize his classes, he made the decision to take a leap and swap out his advanced-level science classes for courses that taught him about marketing research and creative writing. He even took a class just for fun and learned how to illustrate. Carlos' 5Ws were evolving, and the question that became more prominent in his mind was what he wanted to do after graduation. His hope was that taking different classes would open his mind to new opportunities, and it did.

It takes extra effort to enroll in classes that aren't related to your major, but when you feel compelled to do so, follow your instincts. Chloe thought it might be interesting to learn about the design aspect of engineering, so she enrolled in design classes, and completed the requirements for a certificate in design from her university. For both Carlos and Chloe, these decisions to add variety to their original course of studies opened up new career pathways for them to explore.

WHAT DO I NEED TO KNOW?

When you are in a job, whether it is a part-time job, internship, or full-time position, you will have a learning curve. Sometimes what you need to learn is obvious; it's part of the job and may be technical or related to the equipment or process. Often you just learn by following and observing others. These are the times when it is helpful to be attentive to the subtleties of how things are done and to take note of unique situations.

When Jasmine was just beginning her nursing career, she found that she needed to listen to instructions word for word and observe others who were teaching her. She loved working in the intensive care unit and being a part of the cardiovascular catheterization (Cath) lab. It seemed like such a great place to work. Though they were dealing with life and death situations, people were not flustered, and she got along with everyone. But she knew she had to prove herself, so in her mind, she prepared herself to learn. Given the technical nature of the work, she had to pay close attention and then she was able to progress year after year.

Sometimes on-the-job learning is what you need to bridge the gap, not necessarily formal coursework or training.

WHAT'S IN THE JOB DESCRIPTION?

Each job description lists many criteria for the ideal candidate. As you review these descriptions, it is tempting to think that either you have *all* the qualifications needed or you don't have *any* of the qualifications needed. If you are looking at job descriptions that are within reason for someone at your academic level, the truth is somewhere in between: you have strength in some areas, and less experience in others.

Taking a critical look at the education and skills required for jobs that are of interest to you, determine first whether you meet the academic and training requirements to be qualified for the position. Then, look at the overall responsibilities, one line at a time, and determine where there may be gaps between the description in the job posting and your experience. Then, determine how you can gain the experience needed to be a stronger candidate for the position.

SHH ... NO ONE KNOWS

There are things we each feel that we are not good at. We hope no one else knows or has figured it out. These could be a fear of public speaking, meeting new people, talking about yourself, or not having anything interesting to talk about. These fears could also be an aversion to subject matters such as math, science, or engineering. Lack of comfort with these areas may or may not hold you back; however, they are always at the back of your mind as skills you wish you were better at.

Identify ways you can address these and start to practice so that they become less of a nemesis. Have fun with it!

TO ADVANCE OR TRANSITION YOUR CAREER

As you plan ahead, you may want to consider addressing gaps and taking advantage of opportunities to advance your career. Graduate-level education, unique assignments, and certifications are all experiences you might choose to add to your resume. For example, a nurse may advance their career by obtaining a master's degree in nursing. An engineering student may choose to go to graduate school and obtain a PhD. In the field of healthcare and the sciences, obtaining advanced degrees, even in the form of a business degree, such as an MBA, can facilitate career advancements.

In addition to academics, strengthening your knowledge of your industry and understanding the intricacies of how it works will help you become more effective at the work you do.

If you are looking to transition from one career or one industry to another, understanding your gaps and what you need to position yourself for a new opportunity is essential to opening those doors and being considered.

GAPS IN THE FORM OF TIME

Some gaps will occur naturally due to the time in between activities. These gaps may be in between graduation and a job or between graduation and your next academic endeavor. When a job situation changes, there can be time between one job and the next job.

This time gap may also be due to a decision to follow your own agenda and doing things that are important to you. During these gaps, the time may be used to learn more about the world around you. You might take an online class; connect with people you know or make new connections and discover what others are working on. This gap may be for exploring new ideas or taking action on ideas you have only thought about. This time may even be ideal for volunteering, offering your skills to support community projects, or even traveling to learn.

WAYS TO BRIDGE THE GAPS

You can bridge gaps in different ways, many of which are listed here. They are not intended for any specific gap but can be applied as needed to help you get from where you are to where you want to be along your career journey.

> *Staying Current with Information and Technology*: Healthcare and technology are ever evolving, with constant design advances. This field is complex, but it is imperative to stay current with your skill-sets. Many healthcare fields have continuing education requirements; thus, the education and learning never ends, whether it's formal coursework or on-the-job learning.
>
> By viewing healthcare and technology publications, you can learn about the latest trends in science and healthcare. Chloe has now incorporated this question into many of her conversations and asks, "What does someone with a biomedical engineering degree do at your company?" This helps her glean what is important and what are some of the upcoming trends in the industry.
>
> *Observing Others*: Being observant and making a note of how other people handle the same situation you have been in or you find yourself in can be a learning experience in itself. Whether others respond the same way or differently, you can learn from them. Know that others may be watching you for the same reason; thus, it goes both ways.
>
> The reason I suggest you be watchful is because there are so many scenarios you can find yourself in, for example, if you are working in a clinical setting and interacting with patients. If you had to learn each and every situation on your own, it would take many years of practice. If you make note of situations you have observed and note how others have handled them, it could make it easier for

you to determine how you would respond when faced with similar scenarios.

Create Stepping Stones: As Chloe was trying to bridge the gap between graduation and her first job, she was starting to feel as though she might need to "settle" for something less than what she wanted. We discussed how we might want to shift the paradigm, and that the next step for her career journey is not necessarily "settling" but perhaps a stepping stone to prepare her for her dream job.

I shared with Chloe that early in my career I worked with people who were in some of these stepping-stone positions. They were responsible for many of the basic administrative duties. Today, these individuals are vice presidents and directors in their organizations. Learning at the ground level can really pay off if you are comfortable starting there. The ground level might be an administrative assistant, a coordinator, or specialist role, or a trainee/internship position that some companies offer for new graduates.

Persistence: Bridging any gap requires persistence. When Carlos was looking for a position, he looked online at job postings for weeks, and finally, one evening, he viewed an online posting. After mulling through more than 30 pages, he found a job posting that was just what he wanted, on page 34—the very last page of the job postings. It ended up being his dream job, and he landed an offer.

Saying "Yes" to the Work: Leon, a physician, shared a story about accepting a new position: "I wasn't sure if this was the right move to make. I was newly married, just got back from my honeymoon, and they asked me to take on new responsibilities. Others were given this same opportunity and turned it down. I didn't have much time to think about it, but thought, what do I have to lose?" This decision to say yes has since shaped his life and career in so many positive ways. "Be willing to do the work that no one else wants to do," he said, while smiling. "You never know where this may lead you."

I remember a time a student received an internship offer because she had experience with programming that was hard to find. When I asked her how she developed this knowledge, she explained that she took on a project that her professor needed help with that no one else wanted to do. It ended up being really helpful for her in landing an internship opportunity for the summer. Taking on special projects sometimes reveals a hidden opportunity to gain specialized experience. This additional knowledge can become an advantage.

Accepting the Pause: As Chloe continued on her career journey, she decided to take some time to sit in a quiet space to think. She craved this alone time to consider her experiences as well as all of the conversations she has had in recent years. She thought about internships, classes, projects, and people she's met. The last four years seemed to have flown by so quickly.

After high school, the path to success seemed so clear. Chloe knew which university she would attend, and her next four years were mapped out for her. She had taken all the right steps in her career journey—working hard through school, securing great internships every summer, and making time to apply for jobs.

While the job applications had been submitted, Chloe had to wait for responses. She used this time to continue to meet with people and gather information to fine-tune and validate her 5Ws. Even though this period of time in her life was relatively quiet and not fraught with the hectic pace of life she had been accustomed to, she knew in her heart that she would ultimately find what she had been looking for.

Strengthen Transferable Skills: Leadership, communication, and problem-solving skills can be applied in any job and across any industry. Having effective skills in these key areas is valued at any level of an organization. Involvement in extracurricular activities on campus and taking on leadership roles in student or volunteer organizations provide opportunities to practice these skills. They also provide opportunities to work with a variety of personalities.

Find Hidden Gems: My favorite way to describe special people who have stepped into my life for a short period of time, imparting tremendous help and guidance, is that they are my hidden gems. A gem begins as simply a rock until its beauty and essence is uncovered. I believe that many people in the world have experience and insights to share. Unless we give them a label such as friend, mentor, or teacher, what they have to offer can be overlooked because we meet them only in passing.

I first came to understand the concept of a hidden gem when I was in graduate school. Bill was the technical support scientist I spoke with at a biotech company I ordered reagents from. It just so happened that during one of our conversations, I mentioned to Bill that I was considering a career working at a healthcare company after graduation. Though we had only spoken on one or two occasions, I asked Bill what it was like to work in industry versus academia, and he took time to share insights with me. Additionally, Bill gave me tips on how to prepare for my interview. His help and guidance at that very critical time in my career journey helped me bridge a gap. Bill is just one of many hidden gems I have discovered over the course of my life.

Search for the Right Program: This guidance is intended literally and figuratively. You can choose from many different learning options: in person vs. online, part-time vs. full-time vs. evening or weekend programs. Some training options are low cost or free, especially options online. You can access the formal training you choose to address your gaps in many different ways.

Over time, you may come to realize you would like additional educational experiences as well, such as master's degrees in public health or data sciences, or another area. You may also obtain a PhD in addition to an MD degree. You can choose from many different combinations of degrees in order to gain the knowledge and insights needed for the work you wish to do.

You may also choose to work for a few years and go back to school later. If you take the time to look for the right option, you are certain to find an educational program that works for you.

Recognize Who's on Your Side: Find people who can understand what you are either looking for or trying to accomplish. Leverage that support as you are working to address the gaps. As a physician, Leon is often in a position interacting with students. He advises students of what might be an inevitable scenario at some point in their careers.

"During the course of making decisions around your career and next steps, the reality is that there will always be someone who has more. They started earlier. They went to better schools. They are stronger in math, or science, or research. It is easy to feel like you simply can't do something." He encourages students to "be open to what the possibilities are. Sometimes even your own family or friends will question your ability to do what you dream of doing. If you have a dream and aspiration for yourself, find those who can offer you support and encouragement and hold onto your dream."

DIG IN AND DIG DEEP

Though some of Chloe's classmates were going to graduate school, she wanted to get a job and start putting her skills to work. She wanted to see what she could do and how far she could go with what she had already worked so hard to accomplish. First, Chloe had to find job descriptions that were of interest to her. She thought it would be easy. After all, over the years, she had seen many job postings for biomedical engineers. But now that she was actually looking to apply for positions, the descriptions associated with the job postings she found were not exactly what she was looking for. As we discussed her interests and how she wanted to apply her biomedical engineering training, her search became more targeted.

It turns out Chloe wanted to leverage her biomedical engineering experience along with her coursework in design. She also wanted a position that was less technical and provided more opportunities to work with patients and interact with people. At first, these positions seemed nonexistent, but she was certain there were jobs of this nature somewhere, but where would she find these? She started to dig in.

Rather than looking exclusively at the job titles, she started looking at the websites of companies that did the type of work she found interesting. That opened the door for her search. After she found one opportunity, she was able to recognize and look for other positions that were similar. It turns out that even though she was a biomedical engineering major, the type of opportunities she was seeking had titles that alluded to patient experience. It made sense because her internships involved working on design projects to make healthcare products easier for patients to use.

These jobs involved a combination of technical and business skills along with working with teams in a product manager type of role. As she was looking at the job descriptions, she realized there was a gap. She felt comfortable with the technical acumen needed for the position, but as for the business skills, she was less certain she had the requisite experience.

Now it was time to dig deep. Her time in school had been largely focused on coursework required for her major. Her internship experiences were research and technical in nature. Chloe had to think to herself and remember what else she had done. Remembering that she had worked in an administrative role on campus, she was able to use this work as an example of how she interacted with customers and demonstrated strong interpersonal skills. She then remembered that for one of her internship projects, she, along with the design engineers, demonstrated products for patients. As she began to dig deep into her own experiences, she realized that she had more to offer than she first thought.

DON'T HAVE ANY GAPS?

If you don't think you have any gaps right now, and you know what you need to know, then ask yourself if you are appropriately challenged or if you have all the experience and knowledge you need to be where you want to be? Consider Emma, a recent college grad, who felt quite comfortable in her work. She may not have had any gaps, but she finally came to realize that she had been limiting herself and intentionally not putting herself in spaces where she was challenging herself. She was playing it safe and keeping herself small, staying in her comfort zone.

ACTION ITEMS

1. Complete your personal gap analysis. (See template in Table 5.1.)
2. What are some skills you have that people don't know you are good at? Add these to your personal resume—the copy you keep for yourself (as referenced in Chapter 2). Add these to your resume or cover letter if they might help you land your dream job.

TABLE 5.1

Your Gap Analysis

Gaps I Want to Work On	How to Bridge Them	My Goal for This Gap

IN CLOSING

Throughout my career journey, and as I have been a part of others' journeys, bridging the gap has been the most exhilarating part of the experience. These are the actions and decisions that accelerate your career journey. Bridging the gap almost always involves some sort of risk-taking activity. When you identify whether you have any gaps that are important to you, it involves stepping out, doing more than you might have intended, and experiencing more than you ever dreamed possible. The gaps are not necessarily large gaps, but sometimes you just need a stepping stone, or a helpful hand along the way.

6
Progress Leads to Success

It's very satisfying to be at peace with the decisions I made and see how my studies fit together, and are actually relevant to the jobs I was envisioning.

—*Chloe*

We are all different, so what success means to any of us will inevitably be different. Thus, what I can offer are ways to make progress toward that ultimate achievement, which is the feeling of success. When we first looked out onto the mountain range in Chapter 1, you might have defined success as reaching the tallest peak, and in record time. It is possible though that success may also be getting to a point where you have a spectacular view of

DOI: 10.1201/b22077-6

the mountain range. Just like in life, success isn't just about a destination. Sometimes you don't know that you have what you were looking for. Other times, it lasts for a moment, just like getting to a point where you have a great view, and then you continue your journey to the next successful moment. Though success will look different for each of you, I will share what I have experienced, seen, and guided others through on their career journeys.

KNOW YOURSELF, KNOW THE JOB

Remember to periodically do a self-check and review your 5Ws and your six-photo collage that tells the story of who you are and what is most important to you.

YOUR 5Ws

Who
What
Where
When
Why

Your 5Ws reflect what is important to you in your career journey and the course you follow. The images and words you select for your six-photo collage are a reminder of what is most important to you. Reflecting on both your 5Ws and your six-photo collage allows you to keep in mind both aspects of your world: work and life. These can be your anchors and help you as you make career decisions.

Another aspect of making your career decision is to know the job, perhaps as well as you might know your best friend. You will spend a great deal of your waking hours in your chosen field of work or your career. Thus, it is important to know the job or career you are pursuing very well. No career or occupation is inherently good or bad; the question is *it the right choice for you?* To answer, start by looking below the surface, beyond the obvious, to understand the nature of the work.

The first exposure you may have to any occupation may be information that reflects a typical day on that job and you want to imagine yourself in these positions. You might see

- photos of people smiling
- images of workplaces that are impressive
- people who are doing activities that make you feel good

While this is all real and very positive, you will also hear stories about how gratifying their work is and how they have enjoyed doing this work for many years. These are all reflective of one aspect of the job. As you look at these images and listen to the remarks, you can easily see yourself in that space. It is important to hear what people like about their jobs. It is equally important to understand the challenges to be certain you are prepared for all aspects of the career or job you are pursuing.

Knowing the job means understanding what a really good day looks like and having an idea of what a bad day in that position might look like as well.

One of my uncles works as an auto mechanic. Growing up, I would see this uncle quite often and so I would always listen to his stories. On a good day, his customers were happy, there were new models of cars being released, and he was able to leave work on time. Then there were the rough days. He would describe how it took hours to figure out what was needed to fix a car or how he thought he had solved the issue and then the car still wasn't running right. I came to understand some of the nuances of working in an auto repair shop simply because he is family and I saw him often.

When you don't know someone, or you don't have a family member or friend who works in the profession you are pursuing, look outside your circle. Perhaps you can glean insights from someone on campus, in one of your classes, or in the same dorm. Getting to know the job better is about going beyond what you think the job entails and learning from someone close to the job what problems they are trying to solve in their day-to-day work. To help prepare you for the good days, and the challenges as well, learn about the:

- good parts
- less glamorous aspects
- commitment required
- problems to solve

Leon offers these insights:

> A doctor must look at the full picture. The variables make up a complex puzzle, one which a physician, for example, will try to solve with the patient. In healthcare, we don't just tell someone else what to do. A physician will take all of the puzzle pieces and attempt to understand each one individually before molding them together. They will look to see what the effects are, what the treatment options are, and be willing to own their decision. In order to work in healthcare, one must understand, beyond all else, that there is more to it than just giving a treatment. There is a level of responsibility and commitment that goes far beyond the job title. The willingness, the drive, and the determination have to be present.

Knowing people who do the same job that you are pursuing has an advantage and a potential disadvantage. The advantage is that you become familiar with the nature of the work. The disadvantage is that because you see someone you know doing this work, and they are happy, you might assume that you would be just as happy doing the work. Since we are all different, try to understand the reasons that the person likes their work (their 5Ws) and compare those reasons with your 5Ws. It will help you understand where you have similar perspectives and where you may differ.

If you can, understand the nature of the work, the people you are there to help, the problems you are there to solve, or the solutions you are there to create. You may find some surprises, or some things you need to think about and decide how or whether you can handle them. Let's say the job involves working indoors in one building for 8–12 hours a day, five days a week. You work in healthcare and your job involves seeing patients on a daily basis. They are in need of your care and attention. You like the work because it helps people live better lives and it's a good job. Your six-photo collage shows how much you enjoy the outdoors. And so, on the weekends and anytime you have away from work, you may choose to use that time to the fullest and enjoy nature.

This aspect of success involves understanding the full nature of the work, and enjoying what the job involves on good days, and on challenging days. Most people will tell you what they like about their jobs. Ask them what is hard about their jobs as well. As you are making career decisions, understanding all aspects of the job will help ensure that you are happy with your choice.

STAY INFORMED

Healthcare, science, and technology are always evolving. This is one of the reasons healthcare and the STEM-related fields of work are interesting to people who choose these career paths. Do any of your talents or interests align with up-and-coming approaches to delivering medicine and emerging healthcare technology? Technologies are new at one point, and then they become integrated into daily lives and work. What is new today will be established technology tomorrow. Identify and understand the latest innovation in your field as you are seeking your next steps. Try to understand the implications of these innovations on the type of work you are interested in pursuing.

Are there areas of healthcare, STEM, or non-STEM careers or occupations where the need for people is projected to grow due to current or anticipated healthcare-driven needs? As you learn more about the latest trends and the application of new technology and medicines, you may discover opportunities for success if you have an understanding of these fields.

BE PREPARED TO PIVOT

Success means being able to take what you have learned and apply it in other ways and build your current skills. For example, if science classes and working in patient care are not on your list of interests, you can major in any of these areas and still work for an organization that delivers healthcare services:

- business
- education
- engineering (e.g., facility design)
- information technology (IT)
- finance

- law
- communication
- arts or design
- human resources

You could work in healthcare by applying your skills and experience within the context of a hospital, business, or organization that is involved with providing healthcare services.

When I was in college, I thought there were only two options to consider if I wanted to work in healthcare, but there are so many more ways that the world approaches illness and the treatment of diseases, maintaining health and wellness, and healing. As an adult, I have come to learn more about the various approaches—often called alternative medicine—but the reality is that there are many approaches to understanding the human body.

When you think of physicians, for example, what may come to mind are the people you see when you visit a clinic or a hospital. However, many types of doctors exist. Some are MDs, and some are DOs (doctors of osteopathy). Others are integrative physicians or holistic practitioners. In addition to the types of doctors listed in the *Occupational Outlook Handbook*, there are also Ayurvedic doctors, naturopathic doctors, and those who practice traditional Chinese medicine (TCM).

Alternative therapies are available to people who are looking for treatments as well. They include yoga, mindfulness-based therapies, massage therapy, craniosacral therapy, acupuncture, and energy therapies. These types of therapies are practiced by various trained healthcare professionals, and one of them may be your calling.

In addition, some graduate programs are not clinically oriented but are more involved in understanding the data and trends associated with healthcare. These include, for example, a master's degree in public health (MPH) or a PhD in health economics and outcomes research (HEOR) or epidemiology.

Having academic training in healthcare creates myriads of career and leadership opportunities. The hard part is getting started, thus throughout this book, we have explored how to navigate your career and obtain the education, training, and perseverance you need to have the success that you hope for.

All of the academic programs listed previously require time and consideration of how to plan this time. Some people complete all of their education in sequence, one degree at a time. It is not unusual at all for professionals to obtain multiple degrees in addition to a clinical degree (MD/DO/RN). Nurses may choose to pursue a master's degree in nursing or an MBA. Physicians may choose to pursue a PhD or an MBA or even a JD (juris doctor, a law degree) Nurses or physicians may also add an MPH (master of public health) to their repertoire. Though not necessarily required, the additional education adds to clinical, leadership, and business acumen that enables professionals to advance their careers.

Pivoting can involve changing the direction of your career completely, or it can involve taking the experience you have acquired up to a point and then leveraging your transferable skills to build another career.

> Transferable skills are skills and experience that you have that can be applied across any job or industry with a reasonable amount of new learning. Examples include:
>
> - leadership
> - communication
> - organization
> - time management
> - sales

HOW TO PIVOT

Many circumstances can make you want to pivot. These circumstances may be personal or they may be external and beyond your control. The following steps are a guide to pivoting.

Take a Personal Inventory

List all the skills and experiences you have acquired up to this point. You can use your resume as a starting point.

1. What strengths and knowledge have you acquired up to this point through your academic studies, jobs, internships, volunteer activities,

and community service? Please be kind and generous to yourself in this assessment.
2. Take a look at your major, class projects, or work experience. Analyze and separate the experience you have gained into different facets: technical, life science, marketing, organizational, and communication/presentation skills. Identify all the aspects of what you learned.

> Let's say that you majored in computer science and you may have learned a computer programming language; that's the technical aspect of what you know. The project you worked on involved the design of an app for patients with diabetes. In order to do this work, you spent three months working with scientists and interacting with the marketing team to understand the daily lifestyle for someone living with diabetes. Though you are not trained in medicine, healthcare, or the life sciences as a discipline, you have acquired knowledge that you can leverage in work designed to help patients with diabetes, or perhaps this can be applied to patients with other chronic diseases.

By dissecting work, you have done and separating your experiences into multiple categories, you can share examples that are relevant for a given position. You can then leverage your insights from one project into areas that are different, and pivot, while still demonstrating experience in your core skills.

3. Look at your capabilities and your potential to learn as demonstrated by what you have done and start to compare this to the needs of the work that you are interested in pivoting toward.
4. Inevitably, there are things to learn, but you will not be starting from scratch. You will have experience to build in as well as knowledge and skills, at least some of which will be transferrable.

Career pivots or transitions are a natural part of a career journey that might occur when you are in college, right after you graduate, or several years later. It is tempting for people to question or be critical of such changes; however, these changes are much more common than you might realize. In fact, I have experienced and watched others make admirable

TABLE 6.1

Examples of Career Pivots for Healthcare Professionals

Original Interest	Pivoted To	Training/Certification
Medical doctor	Research scientist	Graduate school (PhD)
	Healthcare attorney	Law school (JD)
	Nurse practitioner	Bachelor's in Nursing (BSN) and either a Master's in Science in Nursing (MSN) or Doctor of Nursing Practice (DNP)
	Healthcare administration	Master of Healthcare Administration (MHA)
MBA/marketing	Medical doctor	Medical school (MD)
Research scientist	Medical doctor	Medical school (MD)
Biomedical engineering	Design engineer	Work experience
Life science major	Medical writing	Work experience
PhD life sciences	Marketing	Master's Business Administration (MBA)

transformations along this journey of self-discovery. We often don't know that people have pivoted unless we ask about their career journeys.

A sampling of some of the career pivots I have observed over time is in Table 6.1.

MEASURES OF SUCCESS

Different people have different ideas about what success and achievement are. Just as success and the feeling of achievement vary by person, what a particular person considers to be an indicator of success is unique to that person. The following list of indicators is not in any kind of priority; they merely reflect people's responses to this question and may suggest how the general public identifies success:

Responses include:

- Family and being a good parent, child, sibling, or friend
- Job, title, salary
- Home, health, auto, lifestyle

Other measures of success that people strive for are:

- helping those in need
- recognition for or satisfaction in doing a great job
- guiding and teaching others
- capitalizing on opportunities to work and learn
- developing one's career
- advancing in one's career
- working with likable and trustworthy colleagues
- living in a city they want to live in
- comfort with work boundaries and personal time
- recognition for their efforts
- the flexibility to make decisions that are right for themselves and their family

Measures of success that are less obvious, but that I have experienced and have seen other people enjoy and aspire to, involve:

- Opportunities for global exchange
- Sharing experience and expertise with global colleagues
- Being in a career with global demands
- Ability to work outside of their home country

Other ways that healthcare professionals advance are through global exchange of knowledge and practices. Medical and scientific journals are global in nature. The research data you generate in your lab can be viewed by colleagues around the world. You can also share your healthcare and medical practices globally. This kind of exchange of ideas occurs when medicine and research are of interest among colleagues and professionals around the world.

Each person evolves over time—as partially reflected in the changes in their 5Ws—and so do their priorities and the importance they place on specific measures of success. I remember when I made the decision to move from a science role to human resources. I was able to refer to my 5Ws and how they evolved, not to justify this career move to others but to be certain I was grounded and confident in my own decision. That was important to me. Choosing to work in healthcare provides a great return on investment.

You attain a lifetime of memories and feel a strong sense of accomplishment knowing that you've impacted others' lives in positive ways.

You could make discoveries that may help the world by understanding the impact of diseases, or easing people's pain. You can save people's lives, so it's not just about a salary or the time that you spend working. The impact you may have on one or thousands is much more than you might ever have expected when you started your journey.

Let's explore the possibilities and the potential results of your investment of time and effort. Imagine these scenarios that you could be involved in or leading. This is what success could look like for you:

- Making a child, or an adult, smile for the first time in years
- Helping people feel better, recover from their illnesses
- Saving a life, or saving many lives
- Developing an app that makes it easier for someone to monitor their health or disease
- Providing counseling that improves the quality of someone's day-to-day living
- Creating products that help someone walk or see again
- Exchanging medical or scientific knowledge to learn how to treat a disease
- Designing protocols that improve patient care
- Helping people gain access to more medical care
- Lending your talents and expertise to a medical mission
- Raising money or offering grants for medical research
- Researching the ways in which the environment affects health and well-being
- Analyzing data to understand trends affecting subpopulations

Do any of these ideas inspire you? Do you have ideas of your own that make you want to stay up all night working on them? Each decision you make can bring you closer to what you hope to achieve, so think of everything you do as important.

If we take a positive outlook, people have many successes on a day-to-day basis. Your career successes start with your educational accomplishments, and achieving what you set out to accomplish. If you have enrolled in school, whether the program leads to a certificate, an associate's degree, bachelor's degree—or at some point, a post-secondary degree—what are your expectations for completing it? What is the education or experience you need in order to do the work you wish to do? From a recruiter's perspective, I look at a combination of an individual's education and experience. Success can be defined through three different stages:

1. Day-to-day successes in your life and in your career that enable you to progress. Though seemingly small successes, they add up or create the spark for something else to occur
2. Career successes with accomplishments worth noting that have an impact on your life and how you interact with the world:
   a. Awards and recognitions
   b. Opportunities to work with other departments or organizations
   c. Genuinely positive comments people say about you when you are not present

For someone who has established their career, this is success, and the good news is that each of these characteristics is achievable. Part of being successful is that people notice you and the work you do. When an opportunity comes up, they think of you. A sponsor is someone you may or may not know who believes in you and your abilities, and will open doors to create opportunities for you to learn and grow. On your career journey, people may advocate for you even when you are not aware of the confidence they have in you and your capabilities. For example, they may recommend you for membership on a committee or for a training program that will benefit your career. A professional sponsor is different from a sponsor in the world of sports, but they are still putting their name behind you and supporting your work.

Personal successes come from making career decisions that challenge you to get out of your comfort zone. They change the trajectory of your life or career, and you make decisions that allow you to honor your values.

Success, as you define it, may have to do with work that fits your lifestyle and scheduling preferences, such as working weekdays vs. weekends or day vs. evening shifts. Financial considerations can also be part of your success. Are you in a position that allows you to support your financial commitments? Does the career journey you select provide you with growth opportunities in three, five, or ten years?

For me, success has meant having the ability to shift my focus between work, family, and service, ensuring that I can attend to the priorities for each and still have time for self-care. As my six-squares collage indicates, family is one of my core values, something very important to me. At a time when I was travelling a lot for business, the one expectation from my family was that if I was in town, they wanted my presence at all sports activities. Being successful for me involves a balance of: work, relationships, emotional and physical health, spiritual well-being, service, and time for exploration. When these areas are not in balance, I am not as happy, so I work to incorporate each of these elements into my life so that I feel whole.

I have felt most successful when I am in a position to be able to choose which aspect of my life and career I prioritize at any given time. Priorities are important because as a working parent, I can't always have or do it all. These are some of my "feel good" statements:

- I have the confidence that I have the skills, experience, and ability to learn and tackle whatever comes my way.
- I have enough information and I am in a position to make decisions that influence the situations I am involved in.
- Whatever I choose to invest my time and efforts in, my participation has a positive impact.
- I am happiest when I am involved in improving the quality of lives and able to have an impact on things that are important to me.

Success to me is being able to share my talents to make something better in the world. It's being able to say to myself each day, no matter what I am doing, I wouldn't trade it for anything.

MAKING PROGRESS AT YOUR OWN PACE

Success may involve learning and growing at your own pace. As much as it might be nice to have all the answers you are looking for at one time, when you want the answers, it doesn't necessarily happen this way.

When Chloe successfully landed her first job, she was able to reflect on her guided journey:

> When I was getting ready to graduate, I thought that my path was pretty clear and I was going to get a job in medical device design and continue on

that path. But having a gap in time between when I finished college and now when I am actually starting a job, I think it really forced me to slow down and understand what I wanted to do and what type of company I wanted to be at. It definitely forced me to dive into the process more than I would have if it came easy and I started a job right after graduation.

Chloe continues to share:

> Even though it was definitely stressful to have uncertainty during that time period and have to go through the self-evaluation, in the long run, I am very happy with how it brought me to my new position. I know myself and what I envision for my career a lot better than I did when I first graduated.

Sometimes you may need to press the "pause" button to think through what is important to you and what is the best step forward. There are also times and circumstances under which you may not have a choice, but to wait.

Chloe is so excited about starting her new position as she shares what she learned about timing during her job search:

> It took a lot of effort and work on my own part, but I have a lot more trust in the process and letting things go as they will. It really had to be that the timing of my efforts, met with availability for a role that would be a good fit for me. It seemed like a long time, but I am really happy with the way things worked out. My new position is just what I was looking for.

Some people use this time to explore new options. Others use this time to travel. To be certain your time is productive, plan in advance how you might use this time and define what you hope to learn as part of this experience.

Interestingly, taking this pause is often referred to as a gap year. But what if you are taking this year to build new skills and learn things that you didn't have time to explore in college? What if your gap year was just the next year in your life? Your plans are simply different from others' and you are not going straight from school to a job. Sometimes jobs are not available on your timeframe, and so by default, you may have extra time between graduation and your job, advanced degree, or whatever you may have planned.

Carlos took a year to do things he did not have a chance to do while in college. He found the time to be so beneficial that he encourages students to plan ahead and take time to explore areas they find interesting. The year helped him pivot and launch a new career in a new city. As a new college grad, he felt he had so little to lose, and so much to gain. This was definitely a time for personal exploration and development.

You may have aspirations to continue your education, so success means doing what you want to do, on your own timeline, while taking responsibility for the commitment to your own learning. There are many scenarios when this has occurred. For many reasons, some people finished one degree first, and then years later, went back to school to pursue more training. The education could be advanced degrees or certificates in the same field. It might be a first degree to advance their knowledge and careers or to pivot and move into a different realm of work. Success is accepting where you are at a given time, knowing that you may strive for more.

HOW YOU DO WHAT YOU DO

The ultimate measure of success is the way you do your work and interact with others. What do people say about you when you are not around? There are many measures of success that we have explored, and this one is special, one that you, and only you, can shape. The best examples I can share are the words that were posted next to the photo of a physician, endeared by his community. Those who knew him described this physician this way: funny, caring, humble, reliable, inspiring, energetic, dedicated, generous, determined, innovative, empathetic, compassionate, and knowledgeable. A few additional attributes that will contribute to a person's success include kindness, truthfulness, ethical decision making, listening with an open heart and mind, respect for others, hope, and builds unity.

ACTION ITEMS

Remember to celebrate your successes!

1. Find a sticky-note pad and at the end of each day write one or two of your "wins." Keep it in in a convenient place, such as in a drawer or on your desk or table. Examples of successes that count as "wins" can be day-to-day activities like submitting your paper on time, or they can be big like receiving a call for an interview.
2. Revisit the 5Ws that you listed when you first started this book. Are there any actions you can take to gain more clarity on your career journey?

IN CLOSING

When people ask you what you are going to do after graduation, my hope is that you may share with confidence, your career aspirations: "I am going to continue my education and go to graduate school or medical school" or "I have decided I would like to be a Nurse Practitioner" or "I would like to look for a job" or "I would like to explore entrepreneurship" or "I would like to take a year off to travel or volunteer." By taking this journey and following the six steps, I hope you develop the trust and confidence to dig in and explore the work you want to do and the career you want to build for yourself.

When you discover your 5Ws, you know yourself well, and have identified the commitments you are willing to make. You have spoken with many people and you understand the nature of the work you choose, despite the uncertainties and risks involved. You know you can learn on the job and can tap into your skills and experience to do what is right. You have built good relationships along the way. There are people you trust, and people who trust you. This is just the beginning of your success story.

Whether your plans are considered conventional or unconventional, you will want to believe and know, in your heart and in your mind, that you have made the right choice for yourself. Success means you know how to ask the right questions, you know whom to call when you need help, and you can solve problems. On a personal level, you know yourself, and you understand others.

It is my hope that this book serves as a source of guidance and support as you are on your career journey and that the work you do will make a difference.

My favorite quote comes from Dr. Jeffrey Bauer. I share his hope that "through all the efforts to improve and advance healthcare, we are increasingly becoming responsible citizens in the health of the world."

I am excited for your future and wish you all the best on your journey. It is a journey of a lifetime. May you find that which allows you to contribute to the world around you in ways that are unique to you.

References

INTRO AND CHAPTER 1

Occupational Outlook Handbook
www.bls.gov/ooh/
"Career Info" App for Occupational Outlook Handbook is available for Android or iPhone

CHAPTER 1

US Dept. of Education

Source: U.S. Department of Education, National Center for Education Statistics, 2012/14 Beginning Postsecondary Students Longitudinal Study (BPS:12/14)
visit https://nces.ed.gov/surveys/bps

Employment Projections
www.bls.gov/emp/

Interactive graphic from U.S. Census
census.gov/dataviz/visualizations/stem/stem-html

Translational Research
https://ncats.nih.gov/translation/spectrum#preclinical-research

Bauer, Jeffrey C. "Not What the Doctor Ordered, Liberating Caregivers and Empowering Consumers for Successful Health Reform," Third Edition published 2020 by Routledge/Productivity Press. Chapter 5 *Advanced Practitioners: Health Professionals Whose Time Has Come*. pp. 93–116.

CHAPTER 2

For additional information, please contact your Career Services office to access available resources

CHAPTER 3

Rath, Tom. "StrengthsFinder 2.0" published 2007 by Gallup Press
www.gallup.com/cliftonstrengths/en/253715/34-cliftonstrengths-themes.aspx

Myers-Brigg Personality Type Indicator
www.themyersbriggs.com/

DiSC profile
www.discprofile.com/

Ennegram
www.enneagraminstitute.com/
Occupational Outlook Handbook
https://www.bls.gov/ooh/

CHAPTER 6

Bauer, Jeffrey C. "Not What the Doctor Ordered, Liberating Caregivers and Empowering Consumers for Successful Health Reform," Third Edition published 2020 by Routledge/Productivity Press. Chapter 5 *Advanced Practitioners: Health Professionals Whose Time Has Come.* pp. 93–116.

Index

Academic training in healthcare, 114
Advanced-level science classes, 97, 98
Advanced practitioner, 23
Advancing or transitioning career, 100
Alternative medicine, 114
Alumni, connecting with, 44, 87
Anxiety levels, xv
Aspiration, xv, 2, 56, 59, 91, 123
Assessment tests, preparing for, 41

Basic research, 20
Bauer, Jeffrey C., 23
Business disruptions, 76

Career and family, managing, 79
Career aspiration, 2, 56
Career center, 29–30, 31, 44
Career decisions, xviii, 4, 7, 22, 43, 50, 54, 79, 82, 88, 110, 112, 120
Career information, resource for, 63–64
Career journey, 1–2, 4, 5, 11, 25, 43–44, 49–51, 70, 73, 96, 110, 116, 120
Career successes, 119, 120
Changes, 32, 75–76
Class schedule, 97–98
CliftonStrengths, 64
Clinical research, 21
College major, selection of, 4, 7–12
Communication, 103
Continuous learning, 59
Conversation expanders, 45–46
Conversation starters, 45
Cover letters, 37–38, 39, 64
Curriculum Vitae (CV), 34–35

Day-to-day successes, 120
Day-to-day uncertainty in healthcare and research, 80
DiSC Profile, 65
DIY initiative, *see* Do It Yourself initiative
Doctor of Philosophy (PhD), 22
Do It Yourself (DIY) initiative, 57

Enneagram Personality Test, 65
Enthusiasm, 87
Experiential learning, 57–59
  and preferences in action, 60–63
Exploring options, 20

Family and work life, managing, 79
Financial considerations, 120
5Ws, 4, 60, 74, 76, 77
  building, 18
  discovering, 5
  what, 6–7
  when, 16–17
  where, 15–16
  who, 5–6
  why, 17–18
  monitoring 5Ws as they evolve, 18
  self-checking and reviewing, 110–113
Freshman, xv, 3, 4

Gallop's CliftonStrengths, 64
Gaps, 96–97, 106
  in form of time, 100–101
  time gap, 100
  ways to bridge, 101–105
Geographic location, 79
Graduate school, 17, 83, 89
Grounded, staying, 75–78
Growth, 95
  action items, 106
  advancing or transitioning career, 100
  class schedule, 97–98
  digging in and digging deep, 105–106
  gaps, 96–97, 106
  gaps in form of time, 100–101
  job description, 99
  learning, 98
  on-the-job learning, 98–99
  public speaking, fear of, 99–100
  ways to bridge gaps, 101–105

129

Harmony, 64
Human resources department, 91–92

Information, gathering, 1
   action items, 23–24
   career journey, 2–3
   college major, selection of, 7
   developing a story, 3–5
   early years, 3
   exploring options, 20
   5Ws, building, 18
   5Ws, discovering, 5
      what, 6–7
      when, 16–17
      where, 15–16
      who, 5–6
      why, 17–18
   job trends, staying informed about, 22–23
   learning from others, 23
   looking ahead, 12–15
   monitoring 5Ws as they evolve, 18
   research, learning about, 20–22
   undergraduate major, 7–12
Informational interviews and networking, 42–44
Internship program, 57
Interviews, 38–40
   basic questions in, 40
   informational interviews and networking, 42–44
   mock, 40
   preparing for, 41–42
   resume writing as preparation for, 35–36
   virtual, 41

Job description, 33, 39, 41, 59, 99, 106
Job postings, 17, 67, 105
Job trends, staying informed about, 22–23

Knowing and trusting yourself, 53
   experiential learning, 57–59
      and preferences in action, 60–63
   5Ws, 60
   learning about yourself through conversation with other, 66–68

learning from past, 68
learning preferences, 59
making time to listen, 69
not my favorite subject, 69–71
resource for career information, 63–64
self-assessments, 64–65
six squares photo collage, 54–57

Leadership, 36, 58, 78, 103
Learning, 98
   about research, 20–22
   about yourself, 66–68
   continuous, 59
   experiential learning, 57–63
   and growing at one's own pace, 121–123
   not my favorite subject, 69–71
   on-the-job learning, 98–99
   from others, 23
   from past, 68
   preferences, 59
Learning curve, 98
LinkedIn, 28, 38, 51

Magnetic resonance principles, 18
Master list, 28–29
Mentors, finding, 49–50
Minimum degree requirements, 12
Mock interviews, 40
Multiple entry points and options, careers with, 9
Myers-Briggs Personality Indicator, 65

Networking, 43–44
   informational interviews and, 42–44
   opportunities, 46–48
NIH translation science spectrum, 21
Non-STEM majors, 11–12, 13

Online employment personality assessment tests, 40
On-the-job learning, 98–99
Original career plans, xv

Personal commitment, xvi, 79, 83
Personal inventory, taking, 115–117
Personal successes, 120

Personal values, 54, 55
PhD graduate program, 83, 88
Pivoting, 113–117
Preclinical research, 20–21
Problem-solving skills, 84–86, 103
Product development, 67
Professional sponsor, 120
Public speaking, fear of, 99–100

Questions to be considered, 46

Research, 20–22
    basic research, 20
    clinical research, 21
    preclinical research, 20–21
Research internship, 81
Resume, 27
    action items, 50–51
    assessment tests, preparing for, 41
    best time to create, 27–28
    building, 36–37
    conversation expanders, 45–46
    conversation starters, 45
    cover letters, 37–38
    first draft of, 28–29
    general resume guidelines, 30–31
    getting started, 29–31
    informational interviews and
        networking, 42–44
    interviews, 38–40
    interviews, preparing for, 41–42
    key content for, 32–33
    mentors, finding, 49–50
    networking opportunities, 46–48
    organizing, 31–35
    questions to be considered, 46
    social media, 38
Resume reviewers, 33
Resume writing as preparation for an
    interview, 35–36

Sabbatical, xvi, 66
Self-assessments, 64–65
Self-checking and reviewing 5Ws, 110–113
Self-confidence, 70
Shadowing someone, 23
Six squares photo collage, 54–57

Skills
    problem-solving, 84–86, 103
    transferable, 115
SMEs, *see* Subject matter experts
Social media, 38
Speed bumps, 70
Sponsor, 120
STEM major, 11–12, 13, 40
Subject matter experts (SMEs), 86
Success, 109
    action items, 123–124
    career successes, 120
    day-to-day successes, 120
    financial considerations, 120
    learning and growing at one's own
        pace, 121–123
    measures of, 117–121, 123
    personal successes, 120
    pivoting, 113–117
    self-checking and reviewing 5Ws,
        110–113
    staying informed, 113
Support network, 87

Time
    best time to create resume, 27–28
    making time to listen, 69
Time gap, 100
Transferable skills, 58, 115
Translational science spectrum, 20

Uncertainty, managing, 73
    accepting uncertainty, 74–75
    being prepared, 78–79
    coming full circle, 89–91
    day-to-day uncertainty in healthcare
        and research, 80
    doing work, 80–82
    grounded, staying, 75–78
    as a part of being, 88–89
    problem solving, 84–86
    starting to ask questions, 86–88
    taking action, 82–83
Undergraduate degree, 22
Undergraduate major, 7–12
U.S. Department of Education
    (2012/14), 10

Virtual interview, 41

Well-defined requirements, careers with, 8
"What" part of 5Ws, 6–7, 78
"When" part of 5Ws, 16–17
"Where" part of 5Ws, 15–16
"Who" part of 5Ws, 5–6
"Why" part of 5Ws, 17–18
Working document, 28

Printed in the United States
by Baker & Taylor Publisher Services